Turning Points

Communicating in English

Giuliano Iantorno / Mario Papa

ADDISON-WESLEY PUBLISHING COMPANY

Reading, Massachusetts • Menlo Park, California • New York
Don Mills, Ontario • Wokingham, England • Amsterdam
Bonn • Sydney • Singapore • Tokyo • Madrid • San Juan

A Publication of the World Language Division

Project Director: Ann Strunk   Developmental Editor: Talbot Hamlin

Editorial Staff
Jennifer Bixby, Claire Smith

Production/Manufacturing: James W. Gibbons

Consultants
Robert Saitz   Charles Skidmore

Design, production and illustration provided by Publishers'
Graphics, Inc., Bethel, Connecticut. Artists: Beverly Pardee,
Joel Snyder, Jane Kendall.

Cover design by Marshall Henrichs.

Photographs: Judith Bittinger, 18 center R, bottom L; Fredrik Bodin, 18
top; British Information Services, 75, 80 top L, bottom L,R; British
Tourist Authority, 79 #3, #5, 80 top C,R; Cecile Brunswick, 108 top;
Civil Air Patrol 115, 116 (all); Delta Air Lines, 95 bottom; W.G.
Hamlin, 12 b,c; Ellen C. Hill, 79 #1; Los Angeles Tourist Bureau, 45;
George Mastellone, 12 e, 88, 94, 95 top; National Oceanic and
Atmospheric Administration, 100 a,d; New York Convention and
Visitors Bureau, 79 #6, 100 c, 108 top, bottom, 109 all; RCA Records,
41; George and Laurie Riley, 18 bottom C, R; Claire Smith, 100 b,e;
United States Department of Transportation, 12 a,d; Virginia
Department of Tourism, 79 #2.

Special acknowledgment is made to Ken Webster, General Manager,
and the entire staff of Marriott In-Flite Services, Boston, for their help
in the development and illustrating of "Food in Flight," pages 94–5.

ISBN 0-201-52154-7 School Spec. Ed.
ISBN 0-201-06318-2
  IJKLMNOP-WC-99876543210

CONTENTS

MEET SUE MACDUFF

CARLOS:	Hello.
BARBARA:	Hello! Is that you, Carlos?
CARLOS:	Yes, speaking.
BARBARA:	It's me, Barbara. Look, Carlos, my friend Sue is arriving from Canada this afternoon. Can you meet her at the airport? I have a dentist's appointment.
CARLOS:	This afternoon? Sure. What time does the plane arrive?
BARBARA:	At 3:20, at Kennedy.
CARLOS:	What's the airline and the flight number?
BARBARA:	American. It's AA 4045.
CARLOS:	AA 4045. Okay.
BARBARA:	Thanks a lot, Carlos.
CARLOS:	Hey, wait a minute! I don't know your friend. What's her last name?
BARBARA:	MacDuff, Sue MacDuff.
CARLOS:	What does she look like?
BARBARA:	Well . . . she has straight blonde hair and blue eyes.
CARLOS:	Is she tall or short?
BARBARA:	She's fairly tall.
CARLOS:	Is she fat or thin?
BARBARA:	Let's see . . . she's thin.
CARLOS:	Okay . . . I'll find her.
BARBARA:	Thanks again, Carlos.
CARLOS:	No problem! Bye.
BARBARA:	Bye. See you later.

CARLOS:	Excuse me! Are you Sue MacDuff?
WOMAN:	No, I'm not.
SUE:	Excuse me. Are you looking for Sue MacDuff?
CARLOS:	Yes, I am.
SUE:	Well, I'm Sue!
CARLOS:	Hi! I'm Carlos. Barbara asked me to meet you. Welcome to New York!

Communication Points

Ask for and give travel information

```
        ] DEPARTURES [

DESTINATION   FL. #   TIME   GATE

Montreal       9021   2:15    27
Toronto         307   2:40    36
London          470   3:20    35
Paris          1015   5:45    20
Mexico City     195   6:55    14
```

```
        ] ARRIVALS [

  FROM        FL. #   TIME   GATE

Bogota          328   4:45    21
Oslo            401   3:15    23
Hamburg        1090   2:05     9
London          907   6:50    17
Toronto        4045   3:20    31
```

Look at the schedules and ask and answer questions with your partner.

A:	When does the plane from Toronto arrive?
B:	It arrives at . . . .
A:	What's the flight number?
B:	It's . . . .
A:	What gate does it arrive at?
B:	Gate . . . .

A:	When does the plane to . . . leave?
B:	It leaves at . . . .
A:	What's the flight number?
B:	It's . . . .
A:	What gate does it leave from?
B:	Gate . . . .

Describe people

Sue
MacDuff
    Carlos
    Mr.
Day
    Mrs.
MacDuff
    Mr.
MacDuff
    Mr.
Cooper

Height: ___tall___

Build: ___thin___

Hair: ___straight___

Color of hair: ___blonde___

Color of eyes: ___blue___

Distinguishing marks: ___glasses___

Height: ___tall___

Build: ___thin___

Hair: ___curly___

Color of hair: ___brown___

Color of eyes: ___brown___

Distinguishing marks: ___beard___

1. Write descriptions of these people on your paper.

Carlos

Mr. Cooper

Mrs. MacDuff

Mr. MacDuff

2. Read these dialogues about Sue and Mr. Day. Then make similar dialogues about the other people.

> A: What does Sue look like?
> B: She's tall and thin. She has straight blonde hair and blue eyes. She wears glasses.

> A: What does Mr. Day look like?
> B: He's tall and thin. He has curly brown hair and brown eyes. He has a beard but no mustache.

Language Points

Open dialogue

Talk to Barbara.

BARBARA: Hello! How are you?

YOU: . . . .

BARBARA: Listen, can you do me a favor?

YOU: . . . .

BARBARA: My friend is arriving from Canada. Can you meet her at the airport?

YOU: . . . .

BARBARA: It arrives at 3:20.

YOU: . . . .

BARBARA: It's AA 4045. Thanks a lot. See you later. Bye.

Listening

Make a chart like this, and fill it in as you listen to the conversation.

NEW YORK Departures	CHICAGO Arrivals
???	???
???	???
???	???

Practice Points

1. **Use the schedules and models on page 2 to write four short dialogues on your paper. Write the times in words.**
2. **Write a short description on your paper of each of the people on page 3.**
3. **You are in New York on vacation, and a friend of yours is arriving from your country. Call Carlos and ask him to meet your friend at the airport. Complete the dialogue on your paper.**

CARLOS: Hello.

YOU: . . . .

CARLOS: Oh, hi.

YOU: . . . .

CARLOS: What time does the plane arrive?

YOU: . . . .

CARLOS: Okay, but I don't know your friend. What does he/she look like?

YOU: . . . .

CARLOS: How old is he/she?

YOU: . . . .

CARLOS: All right. Bye, now. See you later.

YOU: . . . .

Check Points

Communication Points

Ask for and give travel information	What time does the plane to . . . leave? It leaves at . . . . What time does the plane from . . . arrive? It arrives at . . . . What's the flight number? It's . . . .
Describe people	What does she look like? She's tall and thin. She has straight blonde hair and blue eyes.

1.

What time does the plane to	Tokyo Mexico City London	leave?

2.

What gate does it	leave from? arrive at?

3.

What time does the plane from	Toronto Bogota Hamburg	arrive?

4.

What does	he she	look like?

5.

He's She's	tall. short. fat. thin.

6.

He She	has	curly straight	blonde brown black	hair.

7.

He has	a beard. glasses.

Words and Expressions

airline	beard	eye	leave	Let's see. . . .
airport	blonde	flight	mustache	No problem.
appointment	curly	gate	straight	Thanks a lot.
arrival	dentist	glasses	wear	Wait a minute.
arrive	departure	hair	welcome	Can you do me a favor?

NO PARKING 2

POLICE OFFICER:	Excuse me, sir.
MR. DAY:	Yes?
POLICE OFFICER:	Is that car yours?
MR. DAY:	Yes, it is. Why?
POLICE OFFICER:	You can't park on this side of the street.
MR. DAY:	Oh? Why not?
POLICE OFFICER:	Because it's a No Parking zone until 6:00.
MR. DAY:	Well, where can I park?
POLICE OFFICER:	There's a parking lot just behind that restaurant. Do you see that sign?
MR. DAY:	Oh, okay. I'll go there. Thanks a lot.
POLICE OFFICER:	You're welcome.

NO PARKING BETWEEN 4PM AND 6PM

Communication Points
Ask and tell what is permitted

1. Read these signs.

NO PARKING

PARKING

SPEED 30 LIMIT

SPEED 55 LIMIT

KEEP OFF THE GRASS

PICNIC AREA

NO DOGS

DOGS ON LEASH

DANGER NO SWIMMING

PUBLIC BEACH SWIMMING

NO PASSING

PASS WITH CARE

NO TURN ON RED

TURN ON RED AFTER STOP

2. For each of the pictures, choose one of the signs on page 8.

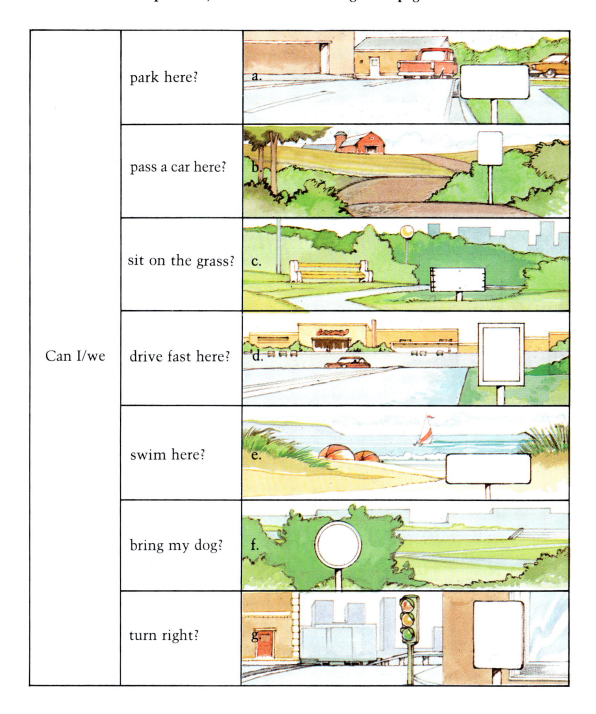

	park here?	a.
	pass a car here?	b.
	sit on the grass?	c.
Can I/we	drive fast here?	d.
	swim here?	e.
	bring my dog?	f.
	turn right?	g.

3. Ask your partner the questions. Your partner will tell you if you can or can't, according to the sign chosen.

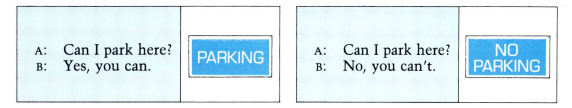

A: Can I park here?
B: Yes, you can.

PARKING

A: Can I park here?
B: No, you can't.

NO PARKING

Ask for permission
Give or refuse permission
Ask for and give reasons

1. Read the following questions.

Can I buy a new record?   Can I visit Uncle Bob?
Can I go to the movies?   Can I open the window?
Can I have a party?   Can I watch TV tonight?

2. Talk with your partner. Ask and answer like this. When you refuse permission, give a reason. Here are some possible reasons.

Because it's closed.   Because he isn't feeling well.
Because it's cold outside.   Because Aunt Flo's coming.
Because it costs a lot.   Because I'm watching the ball game.

A: Can I open the window?	A: Can I open the window?
B: Yes, sure.	B: No, I'm sorry.
A: Thank you.	A: Why not?
B: You're welcome.	B: Because it's cold outside.

Ask and tell if something is possible

Match the signs with the sentences. Write on your paper the letter of each sign and then write the sentence that goes with that sign.

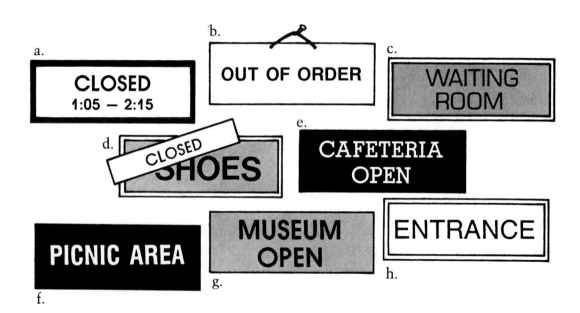

You can have your picnic here.   You can wait here.
You can visit the museum now.   You can't buy shoes now.
You can buy a sandwich here now.   You can't go in at 1:30.
You can't use the telephone.   You can go in here.

Identify things

1. Ask and answer questions using *this* and *that*.

> A: Can I buy this dog?
> B: No, but you can buy that dog.

a. buy

b. play

c. eat

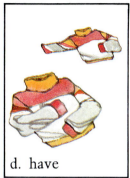

d. have

2. Ask and answer questions using *these* and *those*.

> A: Can I eat these sandwiches?
> B: No, but you can eat those sandwiches.

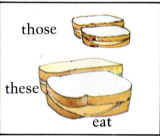

a. buy

b. play

c. eat

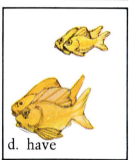

d. have

Language Points
Reading
A COUNTRY ON WHEELS

Cars are everywhere in the United States. One hundred and sixty million automobiles, trucks, and buses use nearly four million miles of American roads. Nearly 150 million Americans have driver's licenses.

To most teen-agers, getting a license is the most important event of their lives. Many students take driver education classes in high school before they get their licenses. Huge parking lots surround high schools to hold students' cars. Young people work long hours at part time jobs to pay for their "wheels."

Many teen-agers like to "modify" their cars. They change them in many ways. Sometimes they "soup up" the engine to give it more "zip." They are proud of their cars.

Millions of Americans drive to work

or to school every day. They drive to do their shopping in large "malls," with many different kinds of stores and enormous parking lots.

The shopping mall is one result of the number of cars in the United States. Another result is the "drive-in." There are drive-in theaters, where you can sit in your car and watch a movie. There are drive-in banks, where you can cash a check or make a deposit without getting out of your car. There are drive-in car washes and drive-in restaurants.

Cars have changed the American landscape. And they have also changed the way Americans live and think. Perhaps more than any other nation, the United States is "a country on wheels."

a.

b.

c.

d.

e.

Talk with your partner or group, and decide on answers to these questions. Write your answers on your paper and be ready to discuss them with the class.

1. The United States has more cars, trucks, and buses than it has drivers. What does this mean?
2. Why do so many people drive to work or to school instead of walking or going in other ways?
3. Where are some places that Americans drive their cars?
4. With your partner or group, agree on a meaning for each of the words in quotation marks. Use the way in which the word is used to help you determine the meaning. The words are: "wheels," "modify," "soup-up," "zip," "malls," and "drive-in."

Reading road signs

1. **Look at the road signs with your partner, and match each one with its meaning. Use the list below.**

> A: What does sign *a* mean?
> B: Children crossing.

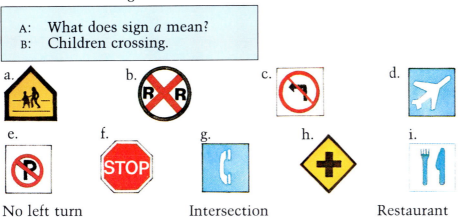

a. b. c. d.

e. f. g. h. i.

No left turn	Intersection	Restaurant
Stop before entering	No parking	Airport
Children crossing	Telephone	Train crossing

2. **Copy the following sentences and draw an appropriate sign for each sentence.**

You can't make any turns here.
You can't drive more than 30 miles an hour.
You have to let another car enter the intersection before you enter it.
You can get on a bus here.
You can ride your bike here.
You can't ride a horse on this road.
The road goes downhill.

Listening

Listen to the three dialogues and find out if people can or can't do what they want to. Write your answers on your paper.

Practice Points

1. **Write sixteen dialogues on your paper like the ones on page 9. In eight dialogues say *you can*. In the rest of the dialogues, say *you can't*.**
2. **Look at the picture and answer the questions on your paper. Use *Yes, I can* or *No, I can't*. (Be sure to write the apostrophe in *can't*.)**

NO BALL PLAYING
NO BICYCLES
NO DOGS

Can you eat your picnic in the park?

Yes, I can.

Can you walk on the grass in the park?
Can you play baseball in the park?
Can you play your guitar in the park?
Can you bring your dog to the park?
Can you sit on the grass in the park?
Can you ride your bike in the park?

3. **Write seven dialogues similar to the ones on page 10, exercise 2. Give permission in three dialogues and refuse permission in the other four dialogues.**

4. **Complete the following sentences on your paper. Each blank can be one word or several words.**
   a. You can't park here because . . . .
   b. You can't visit the museum . . . .
   c. You can't use the telephone . . . .
   d. You . . . open the window . . . it is . . . .
   e. You . . . buy that sweater . . . it costs a lot.
   f. You can't have a party tonight . . . .

Check Points

Communication Points

Ask and tell what is permitted	Can I sit on the grass? Yes, you can./No, you can't.
Ask for permission	Can I open the window?
Give or refuse permission	Yes, you can./No, you can't.
Ask for and give reasons	Why not? Because it's cold outside.
Ask and tell if something is possible	You can/can't visit the museum now.
Identify things	Can I buy this dog? No, but you can buy that dog.

1.

Can	I you we he she they	park here? have a party? buy a sandwich now?

2.

Yes,	I you we	can.
No,	he she they	can't.

3.

I You We He She It They	can	pay. sit. drive. run.

4.

Can	I you we he she they	eat	this that	sandwich?
			these those	sandwiches?

Words and Expressions

because	drive	outside	sure	I'm sorry.
behind	feel	parking lot	these	. . . , sir.
bring	grass	pay	those	
buy	just	side	use	
cafeteria	museum	sign	walk	
cost	open	sit	why	

parking lot

car park

LOOKING FOR THE SUBWAY

3

John, Tim, Carol, and Bill are in Washington, D.C., for the Fourth of July.

TIM: I'd like to see where the President lives.

CAROL: Oh, the White House? It's pretty far from here.

JOHN: We can't walk there. We have to look for a subway station.

BILL: Look, there's a police officer over there. Let's ask her.

TIM: Okay. Excuse me!

OFFICER: Yes?

TIM: Is there a subway station near here?

OFFICER: Subway? Oh, yes, the Metro. There's a station near Massachusetts Avenue.

TIM: Where's that?

OFFICER: It's not far. Turn right at the traffic lights, go straight along that street, then take the second left and you're on Massachusetts Avenue.

TIM: I see. Right at the traffic lights, then the second left.

OFFICER: That's right. The Metro station is on the left, just opposite the post office. You can't miss it.

Communication Points

Ask for information
Give and follow directions

1. Look at Map A. Ask and answer.

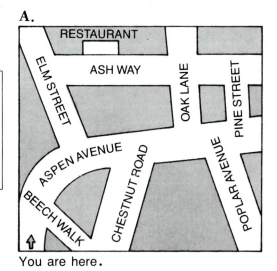

A.

You are here.

	Elm Street?
Excuse me, where's	Poplar Avenue?
	Beech Walk?
	Oak Lane?
	Chestnut Road?
	Pine Street?

It's the	first second third	left. right.

2. Read the dialogue with your partner, and follow the route on Map A.

> A: Excuse me.
> B: Yes?
> A: Is there a restaurant near here?
> B: Yes. Take the first left and then the first right. The restaurant's on your left.
> A: Thank you.

3. Any of the buildings on Map B can be a hotel or a movie theater or a supermarket. Choose where to put them, but do not tell your partner where they are. Give your partner directions to get to each of the places. Then change roles.

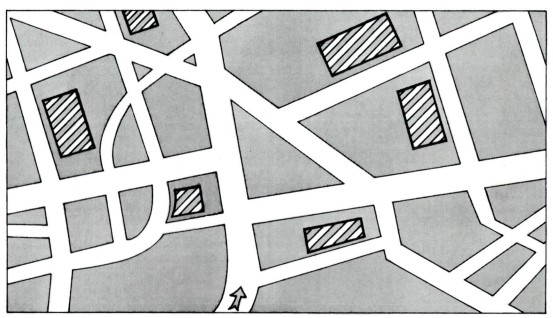

B.   You are here.

Language Points
Game

WALKING IN WASHINGTON

Play a game with your partner. Choose a place on the map, but don't tell your partner what it is. Tell your partner how to get to that place from Pershing Square, near the White House. See if your partner can follow your directions and get to the place you chose. Then change roles.

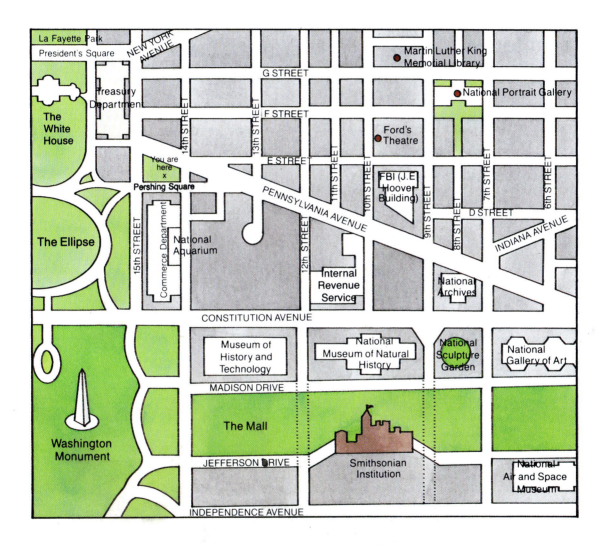

A: Walk along Pennsylvania Avenue to 7th Street. Turn right on 7th Street and take your third left onto Jefferson Drive. What building is on your right?

B: The National Air and Space Museum.

Reading

Read "Independence Day." Then discuss the questions below with your partner and write your answers on your paper.

INDEPENDENCE DAY

Independence Day, July 4, is the birthday of the United States. It celebrates the signing of the Declaration of Independence from England in 1776.

There are parades and band concerts everywhere. Some towns have "field days" with baseball games, races, contests, and lots of food. People sit at long tables and eat hamburgers, fried chicken and hot dogs. There is watermelon for dessert. Many families have parties in the backyard where they serve salmon or steak cooked over charcoal.

Fireworks are the exciting end of the big day. After dark great displays of skyrockets fill the air with color. Everyone gasps as the rockets explode into beautiful falling stars.

The Fourth of July is a special day for Americans. It is their own day of pride. There are other national holidays, but Independence Day was the first one. When the United States began, it was a new kind of country in the world. When they celebrate its birthday in cities, towns and villages, Americans are proud that they still have this kind of country.

© George & Laurie Riley

© George & Laurie Riley

1. Why is Independence Day an important holiday for Americans?

2. What important holidays do you have in your country? Is any of them like Independence Day in the United States?

3. Describe one of your holidays. How do people celebrate it? What do they do? What do they eat?

Listening

Listen to the old pirate Harry Blood giving directions to find a buried treasure. Follow the route on the map with your finger.

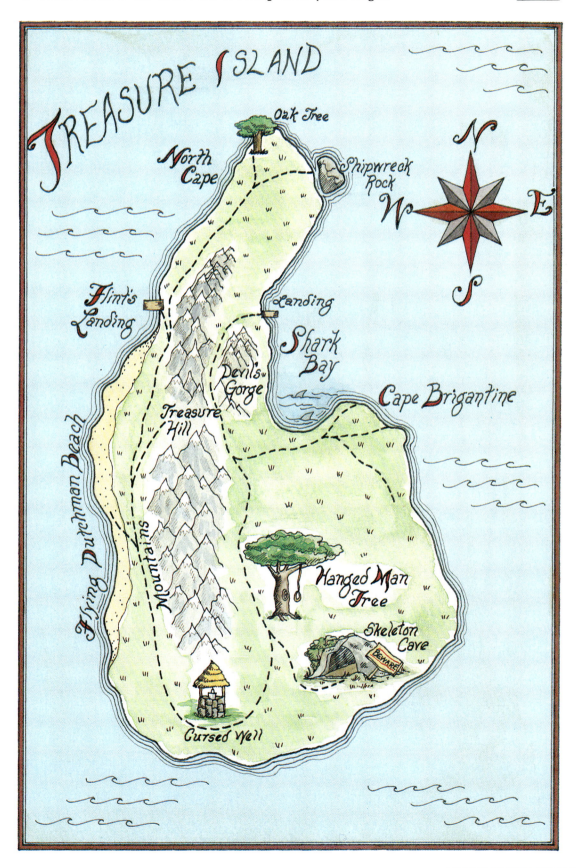

Practice Points

1. **Copy and complete the following dialogues on your paper, using expressions from the box. Each expression can be used only once. Check your dialogues for correct punctuation.**

    a. —. . . , can you tell me how to get to the White House?
       —Go down Pennsylvania Avenue to Executive Avenue. . . . .
       —Thank you.
       —. . . .
    b. —Sorry, you can't park here.
       —Why not?
       —Because it's a . . . .
    c. —Sure, I can meet him. But . . . ! I don't know the flight number!
       —It's American 404.
       —And I've never met your friend. . . . ?
       —He's tall and thin with black hair and a mustache and beard. He wears glasses.
       —Okay, I'll find him.
       —. . . . Bye.

What does he look like	no parking zone	See you later
Thanks a lot	wait a minute	Excuse me
You can't miss it	You're welcome	

2. **Look at the map on page 17 and write three dialogues based on the following situations:**

    a. You are on Constitution Avenue at 12th Street. A tourist asks you how to get to the J. E. Hoover Building on E Street at 10th Street.
    b. You are on Independence Avenue at 7th Street. A tourist asks you how to get to the National Gallery of Art on Constitution Avenue at 6th Street.
    c. You are on Constitution Avenue at 14th Street. A tourist asks you how to get to the White House.

3. **On your paper, write a note to your partner, telling him or her how to get to your house from the school.**

Check Points

Communication Points

Ask for information	Where's Elm Street?
Give and follow directions	It's the first right.
	It's the second left.
	The restaurant's on the right.

1.

Is there a	restaurant movie theater subway station	near here?

2.

Take the	first second third	left. right.

3.

The	restaurant movie theater subway station	is on the	left. right.

Words and Expressions

			Ordinal Numbers	
along	lane	right		It's pretty far.
building	left	take	first	You can't miss it.
end	onto	traffic light	second	
get	opposite		third	

Sing a song!

THE YANKEE DOODLE BOY by George M. Cohan

I'm a Yan - kee Doo - dle Dan - dy, A Yan - kee

Doo - dle, do or die; _____ A real live neph - ew of my

Un - cle Sam's, Born on the Fourth of Ju - ly. _____ I've

got a Yan - kee Doo - dle sweet heart She's my

Yan - kee Doo - dle joy. _____ Yan - kee Doo - dle came to Lon - don,

Just to ride the po - nies, I am a Yan - kee Doo - dle boy. _____

④ AT THE POST OFFICE

CLERK: Hello. Can I help you?

TIM: Yes. How much does it cost to send a letter to England?

CLERK: Airmail is 44 cents.

TIM: How about a postcard by airmail?

CLERK: 33 cents.

TIM: Okay. Can I have two 33 cent stamps and one 44, please.

CLERK: That's one dollar and ten cents.

TIM: Okay. Here's two dollars.

CLERK: Here's your change. The mail slot's over there, behind you.

TIM: Thank you.

CLERK: Bye. Hey, don't forget your letter! The stamp has to go on the letter. Stamps and letters have to travel together!

Communication Points
Ask and tell how much things cost

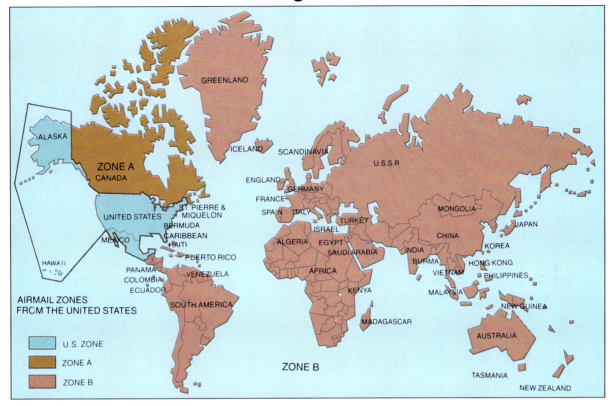

1. **This map shows airmail zones with different postal rates from the United States. Find the airmail zone for each of these countries, and write it on your paper.**

Australia	Colombia	England	Israel	Mexico	Saudi Arabia
Bermuda	Ecuador	Haiti	Italy	New Zealand	U.S.S.R.
Canada	France	India	Japan	Panama	Venezuela

2. **Look at the chart of rates for letters and postcards to each zone. Then ask and answer questions about these rates.**

AIRMAIL RATES

	Letters	Postcards
United States and Mexico	25¢	15¢
Zone A	30¢	21¢
Zone B	45¢	36¢

A: How much does it cost to send a | letter / postcard | to | France? / Haiti?   B: 45 cents. / 36 cents.

A: Okay, a | 45 cent / 36 cent | stamp, please.

Locate places

1. Read the dialogues with your partner.

2. Use the map to ask and answer questions.

> A: Excuse me. Where's the bank?
> B: It's over there, beside the drugstore.

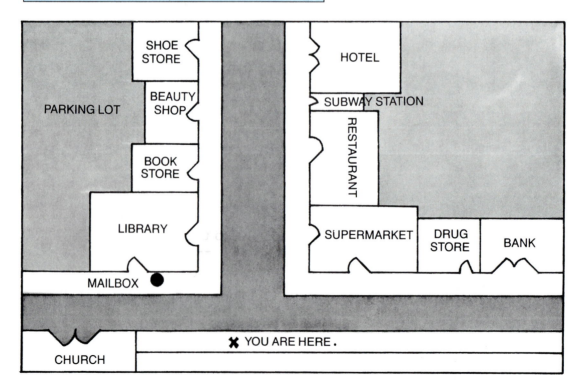

State obligations

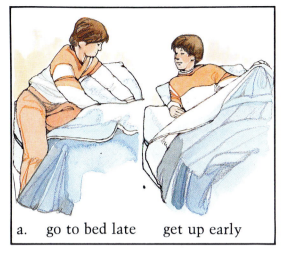

a. go to bed late   get up early

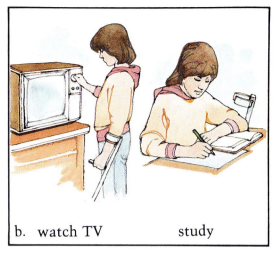

b. watch TV   study

c. use the elevator   use the stairs

d. listen to music   make dinner

e. go jogging   clean the house

f. go to the movies   wash the car

Look at the pictures and ask and answer questions like this.

A: Why can't he go to bed late?
B: He has to get up early.

A: Why can't you watch TV?
B: I have to study.

Language Points

Reading

THE PONY EXPRESS

The Pony Express is one of the most exciting stories in American history. Although it lasted only a short time, people still remember the daring riders who carried the mail across the country on horseback.

Until 1860, cross-country mail moved only by stagecoach or ship. It took at least four weeks for news to cross the continent. In that year, a company called Russell, Majors, and Waddell bought 500 fast Indian ponies and built 190 stations along a 1966 mile route from St. Joseph, Missouri, to Sacramento, California. They hired about 80 courageous riders, including "Buffalo Bill" Cody and "Pony Bob" Haslan. These men carried the mail. Each man rode about 75 miles and changed his pony at each station, about every ten miles.

The riders faced danger and discomfort. Human beings and wild animals attacked them. The route crossed mountain ranges, deserts, and wide rivers. Many riders were hurt. But only once did the mail not get through.

The first mail pouch left St. Joseph on April 3, 1860 and reached Sacramento in ten days. Later trips were made in eight or nine days. The fastest trip, made in 1861, took only seven days.

The Pony Express lasted less than two years, however. In October, 1861, the Western Union Telegraph Company started telegraph service across the continent. News could now cross from coast to coast by wire. Soon the Pony Express was only a memory—and a bad dream to Russell, Majors, and Waddell, who lost $200,000.

The Thomas Gilcrease Institute of American History and Art, Tulsa, Oklahoma

Copy and complete these paragraphs on your paper.

In . . . , Russell . . . , and . . . founded the . . . . The service connected . . . Missouri, to . . . , . . . , along a route that was . . . miles long.

There were about . . . riders who rode fast . . . . The horses were changed every . . . . The riders faced . . . and . . . .

The first . . . pouch reached Sacramento in . . . . . . , but the fastest trip took only . . . days.

The Pony Express lasted until . . . , . . . , when the . . . started operation.

Practice Points

1. **How much do these stamps cost? Write your answer in words on your paper.**

2. **Write short dialogues on your paper for each place on the map. Use *behind, opposite, between, beside*.**

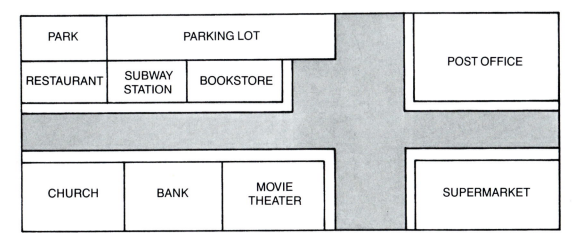

> A: Excuse me. Where's the movie theater?
> B: It's over there, beside the bank.

3. Match each sentence in column A with a sentence in column B. Then write both sentences on your paper:

> She can't go to bed late. She has to go to school tomorrow.

	A		B
a.	She can't go to bed late.	h.	He has to use the stairs.
b.	Don't play the piano.	i.	You have to study.
c.	He can't use the elevator.	j.	I have to go to bed early.
d.	I can't watch TV.	k.	She has to go by bus.
e.	You can't go jogging.	l.	I have to work.
f.	It's late; she can't walk to school.	m.	I have to listen to the teacher.
g.	Don't talk.	n.	She has to go to school tomorrow.

4. Copy and complete the open dialogue on your paper. Check your copy for correct punctuation and spelling.

TIM: Hello, my name's Tim.

YOU: . . . .

TIM: Oh, are you American?

YOU: . . . .

TIM: Where do you come from? Which town?

YOU: . . . .

TIM: I'm from London, in England. By the way, is there a post office near here?

YOU: . . . .

TIM: Thank you.

(Later, at the post office)

TIM: Good morning.

CLERK: . . . .

TIM: How much does it cost to send a postcard to England by airmail?

CLERK: . . . .

TIM: And a letter?

CLERK: . . . .

TIM: Okay. Give me two stamps, please, one for the letter and one for the postcard.

CLERK: . . . .

TIM: Here's a dollar.

CLERK: . . . .

TIM: Thank you. Goodbye.

CLERK: . . . .

Check Points

Communication Points

Ask and tell how much things cost	How much does it cost to send a letter to England?
Locate places	Excuse me. Where's the mailbox?
	It's over there, on the other side of the street.
State obligation	Why can't you go to bed late? I have to get up early.

1.

How much does it cost to send a	letter postcard	to	England? Mexico? Venezuela?

2.

It costs	33 39 44	cents.

3.

I/she/he can't	go to bed late. drink cola.
Don't	use the elevator.

4.

I/you have to	get up early. drink milk.
She/he has to	use the stairs.

5.

Where's the	church? supermarket? library?

6.

It's	down there, over there,	on	this the other	side of the street.

Words and Expressions

airmail	church	jogging	stamps	Can I help you?
bank	drugstore	mailbox	study	Over there.
beside	elevator	next to	supermarket	
between	forget	other	together	
change	fresh	postcard	travel	
		stairs		

elevator	lift
mailbox	pillar box

5 TELL US ABOUT YOUR DAY

(Janet is a reporter for her school newspaper. She is interviewing Kevin Carlton, a famous soccer player.)

JANET: Our readers want to know all about you, Kevin. Tell us about your day.

KEVIN: Well, I always get up at 5:30.

JANET: Five thirty? That's early! What time do you go to the stadium?

KEVIN: At 8:30 in the morning and again at 3:00 in the afternoon.

JANET: Twice a day?

KEVIN: Yes. The training's very hard. It takes about six hours a day.

JANET: When do you eat?

KEVIN: I have breakfast at 7:00, lunch at 1:00, and dinner about 7:30.

JANET: What do you usually eat?

KEVIN: Meat, fish, vegetables, a lot of fruit, eggs, and salad, of course. I need a lot of vitamins!

JANET: What do you usually drink?

KEVIN: Well, I usually drink milk at every meal, but sometimes I have a glass of cider.

JANET: I see. What do you do in your spare time, Kevin?

KEVIN: Lots of things! I swim, and I watch TV. But my real hobby is collecting model cars.

JANET: Well, it's been very nice talking to you, Kevin. Thank you for your time.

KEVIN: My pleasure.

Communication Points
Describe daily routines

1. **Look at the charts, and answer the questions on your paper. The first one is done for you.**

	Sun.	Mon.	Tue.	Wed.	Thurs.	Fri.	Sat.
Carol gets up at	8	7	7	7	7	7	8
Carol goes to bed early	√	√	√	√	√	√	√

never	0% of the time
sometimes	about 30% of the time
usually	about 70% of the time
always	100% of the time

a. What does Carol never do?   *She never gets up at 6 o'clock.*
b. What does Carol sometimes do?
c. What does Carol usually do?
d. What does Carol always do?

2. **How often do you do certain things? Look at the list of things below. Then make a chart and write what you do in the correct columns.**

go to bed early
get up late
eat pizza after school
eat popcorn at the movies
ride to school
have breakfast at 7:00
walk to school
speak English in class
play tennis on Saturday

read detective stories
drink milk with lunch
have dinner at 6:00
eat salads
watch TV in the evening
eat fresh fruit
read comic books
have lunch at 2:00
do homework after school

I never	I sometimes	I usually	I always
ride to school	*get up late*	*eat fresh fruit*	*have dinner at 6:00*

3. **Now talk to your partner to find out what he/she does.**

A: Do you get up early?
B: No, I never get up early.
   or
B: Yes, I sometimes get up early.
   or
B: Yes, I usually get up early.
   or
B: Yes, I always get up early.

4. Now use this chart to talk to your partner.

	Actions	Sun.	Mon.	Tues.	Wed.	Thurs.	Fri.	Sat.	When?
Peg	brushes teeth	✓	✓	✓	✓	✓	✓	✓	every day
	goes to the movies					✓			once a week (on Thurs.)
	watches TV in the evening	✓					✓	✓	three times a week (on Fri., Sat., and Sun.)
	does homework	✓	✓	✓	✓	✓			five times a week
	washes hair		✓				✓		twice a week (on Mon., Fri.)
	has dessert								never

> A: When does Peg brush her teeth?
> B: She brushes her teeth every day.

5. Make a similar chart, and check the days when you do each thing. Include *get up early, have breakfast, drink milk, go to bed late, watch TV in the evening, brush your teeth, wash your hair.* Put in other actions if you want to.

6. Use the chart to ask and answer questions with your partner.

> A: When do you go to bed late?
> B: I go to bed late twice a week.
> A: Which days?
> B: On Friday and Saturday.

Language Points
Reading

INSIDE THE NEWS

Does your school have a newspaper? Almost every high school and junior high school in the United States has a newspaper written, edited, and managed by students. These papers have articles about school activities and interviews with students, teachers, and other people. The sports page, which covers student games, is very important. There are also reports of student shows and concerts. And there is usually an editorial, where editors give their opinions on subjects they feel strongly about. Student photographers try to get good pictures to put in the paper.

In some schools, the newspaper comes out every week. In others it comes out every two weeks or once a month. It is the staff that is responsible for getting the paper out. This staff includes one or more editors and several reporters. In some cases it also includes advertising managers, business managers and other people to help them.

All the staff members of the newspaper are students. They don't get paid. They do the work because they like it! The reporters and editors enjoy learning how to write different kinds of articles and stories, and the advertising staff enjoys learning about advertising. Usually there is a "faculty advisor," a teacher who can help the students and answer their questions. But it is the students who do the real work of getting the newspaper out.

Newspapers are not the only kinds of school publications. High schools usually publish "yearbooks," with pictures of the senior class, the teachers, school activities, clubs, teams, and other student groups. There are advertisements from businesses in the city or town as well. Like the newspapers, these yearbooks are written and edited by students. Some schools also have magazines with student poems, stories, photographs, and drawings.

Students who work on a school newspaper, yearbook, or magazine develop a whole new way of looking at words in print. They know all about the work that goes into a publication and about the kind of thinking that the writers and editors do. They know because they have to do it themselves!

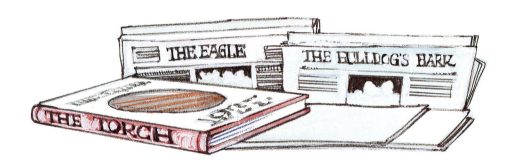

1. **Read "Inside the News" and then write one question about each of the paragraphs. Then ask and answer with your partner.**

> A: What do school newspapers include?
> B: Articles, interviews, reports, editorials, and photographs.

2. **Janet is a reporter for the newspaper in her school. Read the dialogue on page 30 again and write Janet's newspaper story about Kevin Carlton. Tell Who, What, Where, and When. If you use Kevin's own words, be sure to put them in quotation marks.**

Listening

An important soccer game is broadcast on the radio. Listen to find the name of the teams and the final score. In what country do you think the game is being played? Write your answers on your paper.

Practice Points

1. Write the dialogues of exercise 3, page 31 on your paper.

2. Write a letter to a foreign friend and describe what you do during the day. (Use the chart you made in exercise 2, page 31.) Start it like this:

Dear John,
You asked what I do every day. I usually get up at...

3. Write what your partner does during the day. (Use your partner's answers from exercise 3 on page 31.)

4. Read this example:

> Chris drinks milk every day. He plays tennis once a week, usually <u>on</u> Thursday, and watches TV <u>in</u> the evening three times a week. He gets up <u>at</u> 5:30 five times a week, but he gets up late <u>on</u> Saturday and Sunday.

Now write two paragraphs about you and your partner. Use the information on the chart you made in exercise 5, page 32. Start the first paragraph this way: I drink milk . . . . Start the second paragraph this way: My partner drinks milk . . . .

5. Copy and complete the following sentences on your paper. Use *at, in,* and *on.* Use the example in exercise 4 to help you know when to use *at, in,* and *on.* Check your copy for spelling and use of capital letters.

   a. I usually get up . . . 7 o'clock.
   b. . . . Sunday I always have a big meal.
   c. I never watch TV . . . the afternoon.
   d. I usually play tennis twice a week, . . . Tuesday and . . . Saturday.
   e. I sometimes have breakfast . . . 8:30.
   f. I wash my hair once a week, usually . . . Monday.

6. Copy the following passage on your paper and complete it with appropriate words.

   Kevin always gets up . . . 5:30. He goes to the stadium twice . . . day, . . . 8:30 in the morning and at 3:00 in the . . . . The training is very hard, and it takes about . . . hours a day.
   Kevin has . . . at 7:00, lunch at 1:00, and dinner about . . . . He usually eats meat, . . . , vegetables, a lot of fruit, eggs, and . . . , because he needs a lot of vitamins for . . . work.
   He sometimes drinks a . . . of cider at dinner, but he usually drinks . . . .
   In his spare . . . , he likes swimming or watching TV, but his real . . . is collecting model cars.

Check Points

Communication Points

Describe daily routines I always/usually/sometimes/never get up early.
When does Peg brush her teeth? Every day.

1.

I You We They	always usually sometimes never	do homework. brush the cat. wash the car. go to bed late. have breakfast.
He She		does homework. brushes the cat. washes the car. goes to bed late. has breakfast.

2.

Once a week on		Saturday. Sunday.
Once Twice Three times	a	week. day. month.

3.

At	8:30 3:30 7:30	in the	morning. afternoon. evening.

4.

I You We They	have	breakfast. lunch. dinner.
He She	has	

Words and Expressions

always	dessert	hobby	never	swim	spare time
brush	dinner	interview	once	teeth	My pleasure.
breakfast	every	lunch	popcorn	twice	
cider	famous	meal	salad	usually	
collect	fish	meat	sometimes	vegetable	
day	hard	model	stadium	when	

soccer   football

6 A ROCK STAR

HOTEL CLERK:	Gotham Hotel. Can I help you?
CARLOS:	Yes, can I speak to Ultra Violet? I understand she's staying at the Gotham.
HOTEL CLERK:	Just a minute, please. Let me try to call her room.
CARLOS:	Thank you.
ULTRA VIOLET:	Hello.
CARLOS:	Is this Ultra Violet?
ULTRA VIOLET:	Yes. What can I do for you?
CARLOS:	My name is Carlos Ramos, and I'm with the *Evening Gazette.* My newspaper decided to do a story about rock music and wants an interview with you. Can I see you today?
ULTRA VIOLET:	Well, I need to get dressed for the concert, but I can see you for a few minutes. Why don't we meet in the coffee shop across the street? I can be there in about 15 minutes.
CARLOS:	Great! I'll see you there.

CARLOS: Thanks for talking to me. I really like doing these interviews. How about more coffee?

ULTRA VIOLET: Sure. Thanks.

CARLOS: Are you glad to be in New York?

ULTRA VIOLET: Yes, I always wanted to come to New York, but I don't like flying.

CARLOS: I don't like it, either. But I really like going to your concerts.

ULTRA VIOLET: Do you want to go to the concert tonight? I have some free tickets.

CARLOS: Great! That's terrific. I love your music.

Communication Points
Ask about likes and dislikes

a. fishing

b. swimming

c. dancing

d. skiing

e. sailing

f. skating

1. Look at the two pictures below and find out Carlos's and Ultra Violet's favorite activities. Write them on your paper.

Ultra Violet's room

Carlos's room

2. Ask and answer questions with your partner.

A: Does Ultra Violet like fishing? B: No, she doesn't. A: What about Carlos? B: He likes fishing. A: And you? Do you like fishing? B: Yes, I do too./No, I don't.	A: Does Ultra Violet like sailing? B: Yes, she does. A: What about Carlos? B: He doesn't like sailing. A: And you? Do you like sailing? B: Yes, I do./No, I don't, either.

3. Make a chart like this. Then read the words and phrases. Make your own choices and fill them in on the chart.

I LOVE	I LIKE	I DON'T LIKE	I HATE
???	???	???	???
???	???	???	???

a. going to the theater
b. going to the zoo
c. going to the movies
d. going to the park

e. going to concerts
f. going to restaurants
g. going to soccer games
h. going to discos

i. swimming
j. skating
k. dancing
l. sailing

Invite people

Invite your partner to do something, and find out what he or she likes or doesn't like.

A: Do you want to go to a restaurant?
B: Sure, I love/like going to restaurants./No, thanks, I don't like/hate going to restaurants.

Language Points

Listening
A TELEPHONE CALL

Listen to these telephone calls. Then write on your paper the answers to the questions.

Who is calling?   Who is the call for?

What is the room number?   Is the person there to speak on the telephone?

Open dialogue

You are calling a friend in another city. Talk to the operator.

OPERATOR: Your call, please.

YOU: I want to call . . . in . . . .

OPERATOR: Can you spell the last name?

YOU: . . . .

OPERATOR: And the number?

YOU: . . . .

OPERATOR: What's your name, please?

YOU: . . . .

OPERATOR: Is that spelled . . . ?

YOU: Yes.

OPERATOR: I can try to make your call now.

YOU: Thank you.

(ringing signal)

OPERATOR: I have a call for . . . . Is this . . . ?

FRIEND: Yes, it is.

OPERATOR: Go ahead, please.

YOU: . . . .

Reading
THEY MAKE MUSIC!

Question: What has dark hair, dark eyes, ten legs, and sings in Spanish and English? Answer: Menudo. Menudo is the name of the pop music group from Puerto Rico that took the world by storm. (*Menudo* means "kids" or "small change" in Spanish.)

Menudo is made up of five teen-age boys. Members of the group have to be between the ages of 12 and 16. When a member reaches 16, he has to retire. As this story is written, the group includes Carlos Rivera, Ray Reyes, Ray Rosello, Robert Rosa, and Enrique Mar-tin. By the time you read this, however, there may be one or more different boys to replace the oldest members. Perhaps one of the reasons Menudo stays so popular is the fact that it remains young.

Menudo began its rise to fame in November, 1977. At first the boys played concerts and made records only in Puerto Rico. Soon, however, they began to tour in other countries. They visited Spanish-speaking countries such as the Dominican Republic, Venezuela, Mexico, Peru, and Spain. In all these countries,

Menudo was greeted with great enthusiasm and gained thousands of new fans.

In 1979, Menudo taped its first TV series. The shows were distributed throughout Latin America. The weekly half-hour program, *La Gente Joven de Menudo* (*The Young People of Menudo*) is still on TV today. In 1982, the group made a second TV series, *Es por Amor* (*It's for Love*). Menudo also released its first feature movie that year. *Una Aventura Llamada Menudo* (*An Adventure Called Menudo.*) The movie broke box office attendance records at theaters in New York City.

The success of the movie prompted Menudo to visit the U.S. mainland. The group sold out many performances in New York. More than 40,000 fans held up traffic outside Menudo's hotel. Menudo's fame skyrocketed.

Menudo went on tour to San Salvador, Colombia, Argentina, Brazil, and major cities in the United States. The boys appeared on countless TV shows. They made a music video, and were appointed International Youth Ambassadors for UNICEF.

Menudo's records in Spanish and English sell millions of copies. Fan magazines have many pictures of present and former members. Fans flock to Menudo concerts in ever-increasing numbers.

Menudo has proved, once again, that music is an international language. Their story and their triumphant popularity are an inspiration to young people everywhere.

1. **Read "They Make Music." Then read these questions. Discuss them with your partner, then write the answers on your paper.**
   a. How many people are in Menudo?
   b. Is Menudo made up of boys, or girls, or of boys and girls?
   c. How old are Menudo members?
   d. What countries did Menudo visit?
   e. Menudo gives concerts. How else do their fans see and hear them?

2. **Music is an international language. Do you like music from other countries? Write about your favorite songs from other countries.**

Practice Points

1. Write sentences on your paper for each of the people in the chart.

Janet loves swimming and she likes going to parties, too, but she doesn't like going to the theater and she hates sailing.

	LOVES	LIKES	DOESN'T LIKE	HATES
Janet	swimming	going to parties	going to the theater	sailing
Miguel	skiing	skating	going to parties	going to restaurants
Sue	swimming	going to the theater	going to restaurants	dancing
Barbara	swimming	going to concerts	sailing	going to football games

2. Write sentences for each of the people in the chart.

Carol likes dancing and Tim does, too.
Carol doesn't like swimming and Tim doesn't, either.

	LIKE	DON'T LIKE
Carol Tim	dancing	swimming
Ultra Violet Carlos	going to concerts	skating
Mary George	going to the movies	skiing
Andrew Patricia	going to football games	sailing

3. Write short dialogues for sentences *a* through *h* on page 43. Check for commas, question marks, and periods.

CARLOS:	Do you want to go to a concert?
ULTRA VIOLET:	Sure. I love going to concerts.

MARY:	Do you want to go skating?
CARLOS:	No, thanks. I don't like skating.

a. Carol invites Tim to go dancing.
b. Carlos invites Tim to go swimming.
c. Andrew invites Patricia to go to a football game.
d. Ultra Violet invites Carlos to go to a concert.
e. Carol invites Mary to go skiing.
f. George invites Ultra Violet to go skating.
g. Andrew invites Carol to go swimming.
h. Carlos invites Mary to go to the movies.

Check Points

Communication Points

Ask about likes and dislikes	Does Mary like fishing? Yes, she does./No, she doesn't. What about Tim? He likes fishing (too)./He doesn't like fishing (either).
Invite people	Do you want to go to a restaurant? Sure. I like/love going to restaurants./No, I hate/don't like going to restaurants.

1.

Carlos Mary	loves likes doesn't like hates	fishing. swimming. dancing.

2.

Do you want to go	skiing? sailing? skating? to a concert?

3.

I	love like don't like hate	skiing. sailing. skating. going to concerts.

4.

Carol likes	fishing skiing sailing	and Carlos does, too.

5.

Miguel doesn't like	swimming dancing skating	and Janet doesn't, either.

Words and Expressions

coffee shop	love	What can I do for you?	 call (on the telephone)	ring up
either	sail	What about . . . ?		
(a) few	ski	How about . . . ?		
hate	story	Great!		

CARLOS: You know, I was in L.A. last summer and saw you at the Hollywood Bowl. You were great!

ULTRA VIOLET: Why were you there? Did you go on vacation?

CARLOS: I sure did! I spent all my money, I ate like a king, and I came home broke!

ULTRA VIOLET: Where did you stay?

CARLOS: I stayed at a hotel in Santa Monica.

ULTRA VIOLET: Did you go to Disneyland?

CARLOS: No, I didn't. But I visited lots of other places.

ULTRA VIOLET: Who did you go with? Or did you go alone?

CARLOS: I went with a couple of friends. We had a great time!

ULTRA VIOLET: Wow! It's late. I have to go!

CARLOS: Okay, I'll walk you back to the hotel. Thanks for the interview.

ULTRA VIOLET: You're welcome. I enjoyed it.

Communication Points
Talk about vacations

1. **Copy and complete the dialogue on your paper. Use the advertisement to help you. Then read the dialogue with your partner.**

A: When did you go on vacation?

B: Last summer.

A: Where did you go?

B: I went to . . . .

A: Did you have a good time?

B: Yes, it was fantastic!

A: Where did you stay?

B: I stayed in . . . .

A: Did you visit any other places?

B: Yes, I visited . . . .

2. Imagine that you have spent your vacation in one of the places in this advertisement. Make up dialogues like the one on page 45.

Italy

Sorrento. Hotel President. 3 stars. The hotel overlooks Sorrento. It has its own pool, sun terrace, garden and children's pool. Visits to Naples, Capri, Ischia. 14 days, from $400 plus air fare.

Spain

Marbella. Superb camping sites. First class facilities including shops, restaurants, etc. Guided tours to Malaga and Granada. Two weeks camping, from $150 plus air fare.

Portugal

Algarve. Beautiful apartments with class service. Two swimming pools and a safe sandy beach. Excursions to Albufeira and Cape St. Vincent. One week from $225 plus air fare.

They're better now than they've ever been. **World Wide Vacations**

Value for Money
Behind each of these vacations is a guarantee of quality value. Your local travel agent will tell you about it.

Find out what people did

Ask and answer the questions with your partner. On your paper, write your partner's answers and add up the points to find his or her score. The scores are printed upside-down at the bottom of the page.

> A: Did you get up before seven o'clock?
> B: Yes, I did./No, I didn't.

What did you do yesterday?
Did you . . .

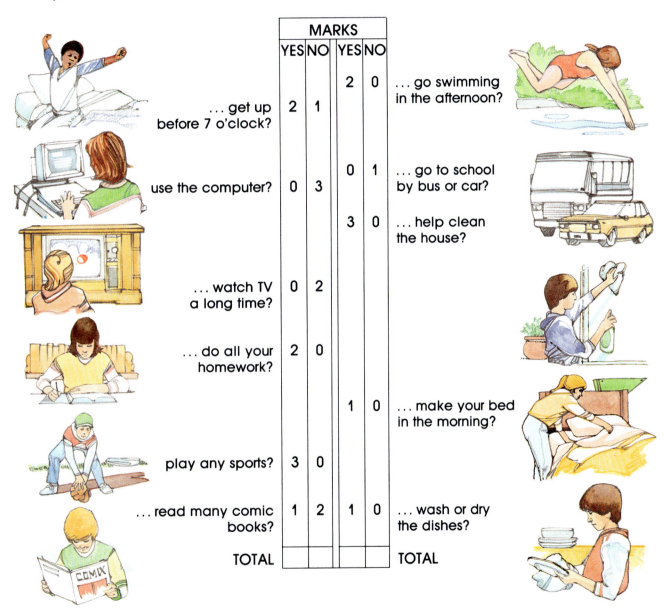

	MARKS			
	YES	NO	YES	NO
. . . go swimming in the afternoon?			2	0
. . . get up before 7 o'clock?	2	1		
. . . go to school by bus or car?			0	1
use the computer?	0	3		
. . . help clean the house?			3	0
. . . watch TV a long time?	0	2		
. . . do all your homework?	2	0		
. . . make your bed in the morning?			1	0
play any sports?	3	0		
. . . read many comic books?	1	2		
. . . wash or dry the dishes?			1	0
TOTAL			TOTAL	

What your score means:

22   That's incredible. You have to be the most active person in the world! (Are you sure you were honest?)

15–20   You are very active, and should be proud of yourself—but take a rest now and then!

10–15   Not bad, not bad. But try harder: activity won't kill you!

2–9   Congratulations! You are very lazy!

Language Points
Vacation questionnaire

1. **Ask your partner questions about his or her vacation, using the questions below. Write your partner's answer to each question on your paper.**

1. WHERE did you go on vacation?
2. WHEN . . . go?

spring

summer

fall

winter

3. HOW . . . go?

by bus

by train

by car

by ship

by plane

4. WHO . . . go with?

family

friends

5. HOW LONG . . . stay? (months/ weeks/ days)

6. WHERE . . . stay?

apartment

hotel

motel

campsite

7. DID YOU visit any other places?

8. DID YOU have a good time?

2. Work with other people in the class to collect information from the vacation questionnaires.

How many people went to: the beach/the country/the mountains/a city/somewhere else?
How many went by: bus/train/ship/car/plane/some other way?
How many went: with family/with friends/with a tour group/alone?

Write the results of your inquiry on your paper.

Practice Points

1. Copy and complete the open dialogue.

CARLOS: Hi! How are you?

YOU: . . . .

CARLOS: Fine, thanks. Did you have a good weekend?

YOU: . . . .

CARLOS: Oh? Where did you go?

YOU: . . . .

CARLOS: Wow! And what did you do?

YOU: . . . .

CARLOS: Did you have a good time?

YOU: . . . .

CARLOS: Who did you go with?

YOU: . . . .

CARLOS: Where did you stay?

YOU: . . . .

CARLOS: What time did you get home?

YOU: . . . .

CARLOS: Really? Sounds like a good weekend. Well, I have to run!

YOU: . . . .

2. Use the phrases in parentheses to write answers to these questions on your paper. Use complete sentences.

> What time did you get up yesterday? (at seven o'clock)
>
> *I got up at seven o'clock.*

a. Where did you go in the morning? (to school)
b. How did you go? (by bus)
c. How long did you stay at school? (four hours)
d. When did you come back? (at 1:30)
e. What did you do after lunch? (my homework)
f. How long did you study? (three hours)
g. When did you go to bed? (at eleven o'clock)

3. Write questions on your paper to go with these answers.

    a. . . . ? I went to France.
    b. . . . ? Last summer in July.
    c. . . . ? I went by plane.
    d. . . . ? I went with my family.
    e. . . . ? We stayed for three weeks.
    f. . . . ? We stayed in hotels.
    g. . . . ? Yes, we visited Belgium and the Netherlands.

4. Use the chart below to write twenty questions. Then write answers to the questions.

you	go swimming	after lunch
Bill	have a good time	last summer
Tim and Miguel	go to the movies	in the morning
your father	go on vacation	in the afternoon
Tim	watch TV	last Saturday
they	play tennis	last night
Carol	wash the car	yesterday evening
Mom	get up late	last week
Barbara and Carlos	go to school	yesterday

Check Points

Communication Points

Talk about vacations

When did you go on vacation?
Last summer.
Where did you go?
I went to California.
Did you have a good time?
Yes, it was fantastic.
Where did you stay?
I stayed in a motel.
Did you visit any other places?
Yes, I visited . . . .

Find out what people did

Did you get up before seven o'clock?
Yes, I did./No, I didn't.

1.
Where did you go on vacation?

2.
I went to	California. Mexico. Italy.

3.
When did you go?

4.
I went in the	spring. summer. fall. winter.

5.
How long did you stay?

6.
Did you	get up have a rest	before seven o'clock? after lunch?

7.
Yes, I did.
No, I didn't.

Words and Expressions

any	fall	mountain	vacation	Make the bed.
apartment	guided tour	plane	weekend	
beach	hotel	ship	winter	
clean	last	sports		
campsite	money	spring		
dry	motel	summer		

vacation	holiday
campsite	camping site
apartment	flat

Present—Past

am/is/are—was/were
come—came
do—did
get—got
go—went

Sing a song!

THE BOY FROM NEW YORK CITY by John Taylor

Chorus: Oo-wah, oo-wah, come on, Kit-ty, Tell us a-bout the Boy From

Verse:
New York Cit-y. He's kind of tall,___ He's real-ly fine,___

Some day I hope to make him mine, all mine._____

And he's so neat,___ and oh, so sweet,_

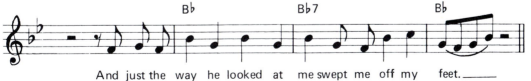

And just the way he looked at me swept me off my feet._____

Verse 2: He's really down, and he's no clown.
    He has the finest penthouse I've ever seen in town.
    And he's cute, in his mohair suit,
    And he keeps his pockets full of spending loot.

Verse 3: He can dance and make romance,
    And that's when I fell in love with just one glance.
    He's so shy, and so was I.
    And now I know we'll never ever say goodbye.

8 AN AUTOMOBILE ACCIDENT

BARBARA: Here I am, Carlos! Right on time!

CARLOS: Good! Come on, get in the car. Let's go. It's getting late!

BARBARA: Say, Carlos, where were you this afternoon? You weren't at home when I called you.

CARLOS: Uh . . . this afternoon? No, of course I wasn't home. I was at the office. I'm writing an article on . . . rock music in New York.

BARBARA: Oh, how interesting. But I called the office, and you weren't there, either.

CARLOS: Of course not. I was in the coffee shop. You know, the one near the office.

BARBARA: You were in a coffee shop, all right! And there was a *very* attractive young woman with you . . . Hey! Stop! The light is red! Watch out!

Communication Points

Find out where people were

YESTERDAY MORNING

a. Carlos

at work

b. Mr. Cooper

at the barber's

c. Miss Bennett

at the hairdresser's

YESTERDAY AFTERNOON

d. Mrs. Day and Bill

at the supermarket

e. Barbara

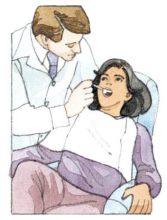

at the dentist's

f. John

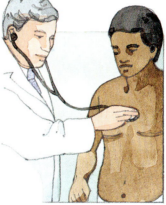

at the doctor's

LAST NIGHT

g. John and Tim

at the movies

h. Carol

at home

i. Barbara and Carlos

at the disco

1. Look at the pictures on page 53 and ask and answer with your partner.

> A: Where was Carlos yesterday morning?
> B: He was at work.
> A: Where were Mrs. Day and Bill yesterday afternoon?
> B: They were at the supermarket.

2. Ask and answer.

> A: Was Barbara at the dentist's yesterday afternoon?
> B: Yes, she was.
> A: Were John and Tim at the supermarket last night?
> B: No, they weren't. They were at the movies.

3. Ask and answer.

> A: Carlos was at work yesterday morning. What about Mr. Cooper?
> B: He wasn't at work. He was at the barber's.
> A: John was at the doctor's yesterday afternoon. What about Barbara?
> B: She wasn't at the doctor's. She was at the dentist's.

Language Points
Listening

1. Make a schedule for a week. Then listen to the tape, and write on your schedule what Barbara did last week and when she did it.

MONDAY	TUESDAY	WEDNESDAY	THURSDAY	FRIDAY
9:00				
10:00				
11:00				
12:00				
1:00				
2:00				
3:00				
4:00				
5:00				

2. Ask and answer questions about Barbara with your partner.

> A: Where was Barbara on Monday afternoon?
> B: She was at the dentist's.
> A: Where was she in the evening?
> B: She was at a disco with Carlos.

Game

You and your partner are Matty and Joel. Work with another pair.
They are police officers. They will ask you questions separately.
Remember, your stories have to match!

ALIBI

There was a robbery at a bank in New York between eight o'clock and ten o'clock on Saturday evening. The robbers stole a lot of money. People on the street described a man and woman as the robbers. Later, the police arrested Matty and Joel. The police thought they robbed the bank. They were questioned by the police. One of the police officers wrote down their story.

Matty Chase and Joel Rush went to the Salerno restaurant at about nine o'clock in the evening. The Salerno is a small Italian restaurant on East 74th Street. Matty wanted to go to a Mexican restaurant and eat tacos, but Joel wanted to eat Italian food, so Matty went with him. They sat at a table for two near the front of the restaurant. Joel wanted spaghetti, but Matty asked for a big pizza instead. So Joel ordered spaghetti for himself and a big pizza for Matty. They both had coffee. The waiters sang Italian music, and Matty and Joel stayed for more than two hours listening to the music and drinking coffee. Matty drank four cups of Italian coffee, and Joel drank three cups of American coffee. They left at a quarter past eleven. Matty paid the bill with her credit card, because Joel didn't have any money. As they walked out of the restaurant, Matty said she was hungry and asked Joel to come and have some tacos with her. They went to the Mexican restaurant on East 75th Street.

POLICE OFFICERS' QUESTIONS

Be sure to use these words in your answers: *was, wanted, sat, ate, had, drank, saw, stayed, paid, went.*

1. Where were you at nine o'clock?
2. Who were you with?
3. Where is the Salerno restaurant?
4. Did you both want to go there?
5. Where did you sit?
6. What did you eat?
7. What did your friend have?
8. What did you drink?
9. Did anyone else see you there?
10. How long did you stay?
11. Who paid the bill?
12. Where did you go after you left the Salerno restaurant?

Open dialogue

Talk to Bill.

BILL: Hello, how are you?

YOU: . . . .

BILL: Not too bad, thanks. What did you do last night?

YOU: I went to the movies.

BILL: You did? What did you see?

YOU: . . . .

BILL: Oh? Where was it?

YOU: . . . .

BILL: Did you like it?

YOU: . . . .

BILL: What kind of movie was it?

YOU: . . . .

BILL: I like the old movies. They're doing *Casablanca* at the World Theater. You know, with Humphrey Bogart? What about going on Saturday?

YOU: . . . .

BILL: Okay! See you then.

Practice Points

1. **Read the dialogue on page 52 again, and write answers to the following questions on your paper. The first two are done for you.**

   a. Were Barbara and Carlos in a bus? *No, they weren't.*
   b. Did Barbara ask Carlos some questions? *Yes, she did.*
   c. Were they in Carlos's car?
   d. Was Carlos at home?
   e. Where was he?
   f. Did Barbara telephone Carlos at work?
   g. Was Carlos there?
   h. Where was he?
   i. Did Barbara see Carlos in the coffee shop?
   j. Was Carlos with an attractive young woman?
   k. Did the car get to the traffic light?
   l. Was the traffic light green?
   m. Was it red?
   n. Did Carlos have an accident?

2. **Write sentences using *in* or *at* on your paper. The first one is done for you.**

   a. Carlos / New York / yesterday
   Carlos was in New York yesterday.
   b. Tim / doctor's / yesterday afternoon
   c. Mrs. Day and Bill / supermarket / yesterday
   d. Miguel / Mexico / last spring
   e. Bill and Carol / Washington / last summer
   f. Sue / Toronto / last week
   g. Carlos / barber's / yesterday morning
   h. Janet and Mrs. Koga / hairdresser's / yesterday afternoon

3. Write short dialogues on your paper using *at* and *on*. The first one is done for you.

  a. Mr. Cooper / Monday morning / (home) barber's

Where was Mr Cooper on Monday morning? Was he at home?
No, he wasn't at home. He was at the barber's.

  b. Barbara / Friday afternoon / (library) dentist's
  c. Tim and Bill / Saturday afternoon / (zoo) movies
  d. Miss Bennett / Tuesday morning / (doctor's) hairdresser
  e. Miguel / Sunday afternoon / (movies) football game
  f. Barbara and Carlos / Wednesday evening / (disco) coffee shop
  g. Mr. and Mrs. Cooper / Monday evening / (movies) theater
  h. Janet / Thursday afternoon / (park) post office

Check Points

Communication Points

Find out where people were

Where was Carlos yesterday morning?
He was at the office.
Where were Mrs. Day and Bill yesterday afternoon?
They were at the supermarket.
Was Carlos at the office yesterday morning? Yes, he was.

Carlos was at the office yesterday morning. What about Mr. Cooper?
He wasn't at the office. He was at the barber's.

1.

Where were	you Mrs. Day and Bill	on Monday this yesterday	morning? afternoon? evening?
		last night?	

2.

I	was	at	home.
We They	were		work. the supermarket. the dentist's.

3.

Was	Carlos Mrs. Day Carol	at	home? work? the supermarket?

4.

Yes,	he she	was.
No,	he she	wasn't.

5.

Were	Mrs. Day Carlos	and	Carol Barbara	at	the dentist's the supermarket the disco	this yesterday	morning? afternoon? evening?
						last night?	

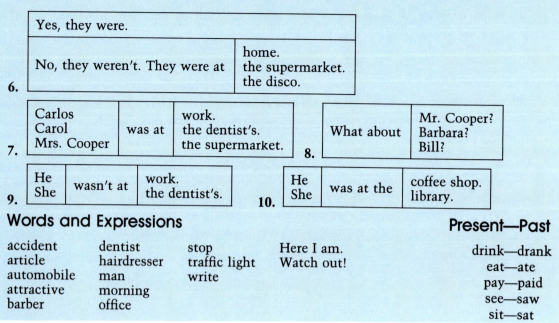

Yes, they were.	
No, they weren't. They were at	home. the supermarket. the disco.

6.

Carlos Carol Mrs. Cooper	was at	work. the dentist's. the supermarket.

7.

What about	Mr. Cooper? Barbara? Bill?

8.

He She	wasn't at	work. the dentist's.

9.

He She	was at the	coffee shop. library.

10.

Words and Expressions

Present—Past

accident	dentist	stop	Here I am.
article	hairdresser	traffic light	Watch out!
automobile	man	write	
attractive	morning		
barber	office		

drink—drank
eat—ate
pay—paid
see—saw
sit—sat

Sing a song!

JAMAICA FAREWELL by Irving Burgie

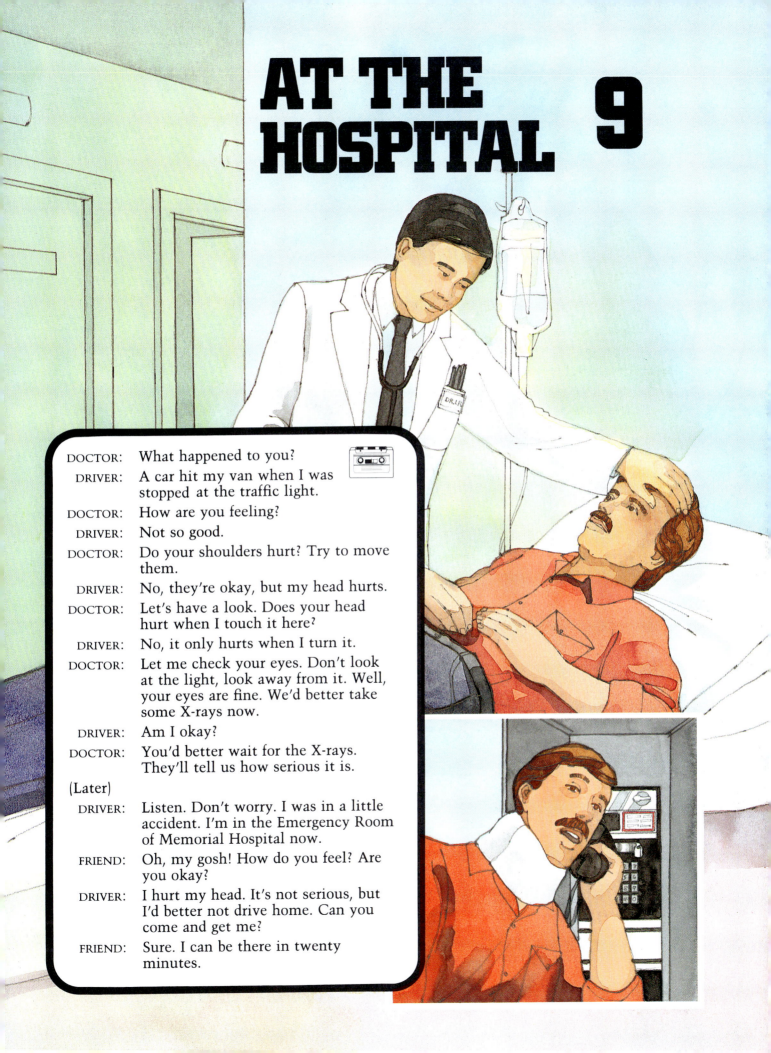

AT THE HOSPITAL

9

DOCTOR: What happened to you?

DRIVER: A car hit my van when I was stopped at the traffic light.

DOCTOR: How are you feeling?

DRIVER: Not so good.

DOCTOR: Do your shoulders hurt? Try to move them.

DRIVER: No, they're okay, but my head hurts.

DOCTOR: Let's have a look. Does your head hurt when I touch it here?

DRIVER: No, it only hurts when I turn it.

DOCTOR: Let me check your eyes. Don't look at the light, look away from it. Well, your eyes are fine. We'd better take some X-rays now.

DRIVER: Am I okay?

DOCTOR: You'd better wait for the X-rays. They'll tell us how serious it is.

(Later)

DRIVER: Listen. Don't worry. I was in a little accident. I'm in the Emergency Room of Memorial Hospital now.

FRIEND: Oh, my gosh! How do you feel? Are you okay?

DRIVER: I hurt my head. It's not serious, but I'd better not drive home. Can you come and get me?

FRIEND: Sure. I can be there in twenty minutes.

Communication Points
Identify parts of the body

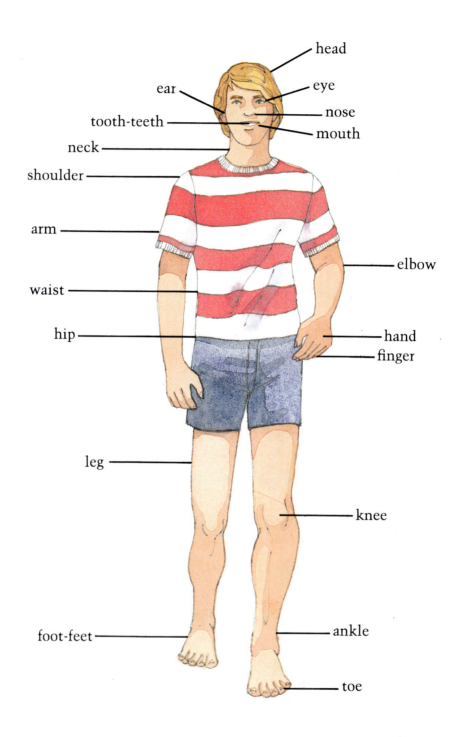

head
eye
ear
nose
tooth-teeth
mouth
neck
shoulder
arm
elbow
waist
hip
hand
finger
leg
knee
foot-feet
ankle
toe

Ask and tell what part of the body hurts. Point to that part.

A:	Does your knee hurt?	A:	Do your feet hurt?
B:	No, my ankle hurts.	B:	No, my toes hurt.

Ask and tell about health
Give advice

1. Talk about how you feel. Use the pictures as a guide.

a. have a headache

b. have a stomachache

c. have a backache

d. have a fever

e. have a cold

f. have a sore throat

go to the doctor

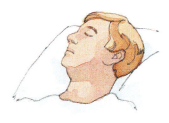
go to bed

A: How are you feeling?
B: Not so good. I have a stomachache.
A: You'd better go to the doctor.
B: You're right. I'd better.

A: How do you feel?
B: Not so good. I have a cold.
A: You'd better go to bed.
B: You're right. I'd better.

2. What's wrong with them?

A: What's wrong with her?
B: She has a broken arm.

Language Points

Reading

USING YOUR RIGHT AND LEFT BRAIN

"I can't remember her name, but I never forget a face." How many times have you heard people say that? Most people can remember about 10,000 faces! We can all see tiny differences in faces, but it is very difficult to describe these differences—to put them into words. That is because the brain, the part of you that you think with, is divided in half. The part of the brain that helps us see the differences is not the same as the part we use to describe them.

Try this with a friend. Find some magazine pictures of similar people, people of the same sex and about the same age. Now describe the face of one of these people to your friend. But part of this game is that you can only talk about the shape of the face and the shapes of the eyes, nose, and mouth. You cannot describe the color of the eyes, skin, hair, or eyebrows! You will find it very hard to put into words the way you tell one person from another.

Scientists are very interested in this problem. They tell us that we use the right half of our brains to look at faces. That is the part of the brain that knows where things are and what shape they are. We use the left half of the brain to give a name to the face we have just recognized. The left half is the language side of the brain.

One way scientists know this is by looking at people who have difficulty using language. Most of these people have something wrong with the *left* half of their brains. They may not be able to find the right word, or they may not use words in the right order. But when the *right* half of the brain is damaged, people cannot copy a simple drawing of a square or a triangle.

Next time you see your friend and say, "Hi, Jimmy," remember, you can only do this if both sides of your brain are hard at work.

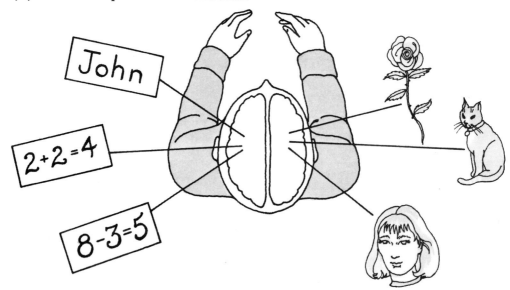

Read "Using Your Right and Left Brain" and answer these questions on your paper.

1. Which is the language half of the brain?
2. About how many faces can most people remember?
3. What is hard to do if something is wrong with the right half of your brain?
4. Can you recognize and name a friend with only half of your brain working?

Listening

Listen to the conversation and write on your paper the name of the patient, what is wrong with her, and the day and time when the patient will see the doctor.

Open dialogue

Talk to the doctor's receptionist on the telephone.

RECEPTIONIST:	Dr. Brown's office.
YOU:	. . . .
RECEPTIONIST:	What's the problem?
YOU:	. . . .
RECEPTIONIST:	Is it an emergency?
YOU:	No, but . . . .
RECEPTIONIST:	I see. What about tomorrow morning at 10:30?
YOU:	I can't come then because . . . .
RECEPTIONIST:	The doctor can see you tomorrow afternoon at 4:15. Is that all right?
YOU:	. . . .
RECEPTIONIST:	Okay, 4:15, then.
YOU:	. . . .
RECEPTIONIST:	You're welcome. Goodbye.
YOU:	. . . .

Practice Points

1. Match the sentences. Write on your paper.

> A: It's cold out here!
> B: You'd better go in the house.

A
a. It's cold out here!
b. It's late!
c. It's hot in here!
d. I'm hungry!
e. I'm thirsty!
f. I have a lot to do tomorrow.
g. I have a fever.
h. I have to go to school tomorrow.

B
i. You'd better get up early.
j. You'd better drink some water.
k. You'd better go to bed.
l. You'd better open the window.
m. You'd better see the doctor.
n. You'd better do your homework.
o. You'd better go in the house.
p. You'd better have some lunch.

2. Draw a monster on your paper. Make your monster have these body parts.

one head	two noses	fifteen feet
one eye	three mouths	six arms
four ears	five legs	twelve hands

Work alone. Then talk about your monster with your partner.

3. Look at the chart. Then copy and complete the letter using *me, you, him, her, it, us,* or *them.*

I	was sick. The doctor saw	me.
He	was sick. The doctor saw	him.
She	was sick. The doctor saw	her.
You	were sick. The doctor saw	you.
We	were sick. The doctor saw	us.
They	were sick. The doctor saw	them.
The cat	was sick. The doctor saw	it.
The dogs	were sick. The doctor saw	them.

Dear Julio,

I'm sorry I didn't write to . . . last week. You'll never guess what happened! A car hit . . . when I was walking across the street. I was hurt, and the driver was, too. He hurt his head. An ambulance took the two of . . . to the hospital.

My doctor told . . . I had a broken ankle. His doctor told . . . he needed an X-ray. We were in the hospital for hours. I called my mother and told . . . about the accident. She was very upset.

Now I'm home and my ankle is much better, but I can't walk on . . . . Tell your parents I'll write to . . . next week.

Your friend,

Jack

4. Now write a letter to a friend. Tell him or her how you are feeling. Use the same form as the letter above.

5. Look at the pictures. On your paper, write the name of each part of the body.

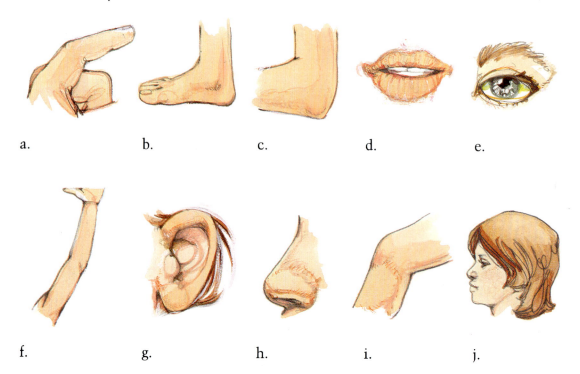

a.   b.   c.   d.   e.

f.   g.   h.   i.   j.

Check Points

Communication Points

Identify parts of the body	Does your knee hurt? No, my ankle hurts.
Ask and tell about health	How do you feel?/How are you feeling? Not so good, I have a stomachache.
Give advice	You'd better go to the doctor. You're right, I'd better. What's wrong with her? She has a broken arm.

1.

How	do you feel? are you feeling?

2.

Not so good. I have a	stomachache. fever. cold.

3.

What's wrong with	her? him? them?

4.

She He	has a broken	arm. leg.
They have broken fingers.		

5.

Does your	knee ankle leg	hurt?

6.

No, my	leg knee ankle	hurts.

7.

I'd You'd We'd They'd He'd She'd	better	go in. go to the doctor. open the window. get up early.

8.

The doctor saw	me. him. her. you. us. them. it.

Words and Expressions

backache	sick	Body parts		
broken	sore	ankle	hand	nose
cold	stomachache	arm	head	shoulder
couple	them	ear	hip	toe
earache	throat	elbow	knee	tooth, teeth
emergency	touch	eye	leg	waist
fever	us	finger	mouth	
headache	X-rays	foot, feet	neck	
receptionist				
serious				

Don't worry.
I'd/you'd/he'd/she'd/we'd/they'd better
Let's have a look.
Oh my gosh!
What's wrong with her/him?

SUE: What did you do last night?

BARBARA: I went out with Carlos.

SUE: You did? What did he say about that woman at the coffee shop yesterday?

BARBARA: Nothing. He didn't have time. We had an automobile accident.

SUE: Oh, no! What happened?

BARBARA: Well, Carlos was driving very fast, and I asked where he was yesterday. He was starting to explain when the light turned red.

SUE: Didn't he stop?

BARBARA: No, he didn't. So he hit a van.

SUE: No kidding! Were you hurt?

BARBARA: No, we weren't, but the other driver went to the hospital. He hit his head, but he's okay now.

SUE: That's good.

Communication Points
Narrate a past event
Ask and answer about past events

1. Mrs. Nelson saw the accident. Complete the following dialogue on your paper. Choose your answers from the sentences in the box. Then practice with your partner.

OFFICER: Did you see the accident?

WITNESS: . . . .

OFFICER: What's your name, please?

WITNESS: . . . .

OFFICER: What were you doing?

WITNESS: . . . .

OFFICER: Were you on this side of the street or on the other side?

WITNESS: . . . .

OFFICER: All right. Tell me what happened.

WITNESS: . . . .

OFFICER: And what about the sports car?

WITNESS: . . . .

OFFICER: Didn't he stop?

WITNESS: . . . .

OFFICER: Was anybody hurt?

WITNESS: . . . .

OFFICER: Thank you. Can you tell me anything else?

WITNESS: . . . .

On this side.

It came from Palisade Avenue. The young man was driving very fast.

Not really. When you arrived, the young man was calling the garage.

Yes, I did.

Yes, the man in the van went to the hospital.

Evelyn Nelson.

Well, he tried to, but when he stopped it was too late, so his car hit the van.

Well, I was waiting for the bus; it was about nine o'clock.

The van was at the traffic light and the light was red.

---

2. Take Mrs. Nelson's role and describe the accident to your partner. The following phrases may help you.

Last night, at about . . ., . . . was waiting . . . . I saw . . . . The light was . . . . Then a young man in a . . . . He was driving . . . and when he tried to . . . , it was too . . . , so his car . . . . The driver of the van . . . , and . . . .

3. Read these situations carefully. Then look at column 1 and column 2 below. Decide which answers go with which questions. Then with your partner make up short dialogues that fit the situations *a* through *g*.

a. You and your family went to a restaurant last night, but you didn't like it.

> A: Didn't you go to a restaurant last night?
> B: Yes, but we didn't like the food very much.

b. Your sister drove to work yesterday. She always gets home at six, but last night she got home late.

c. Your father went to Tokyo last year and saw a Japanese film, but he didn't understand it.

d. You were in a hurry yesterday. When you went out, you turned off the lights, but you forgot to lock the door.

e. Tim came to the party last night, but he went home early.

f. Your mother sent you to the supermarket yesterday, but you forgot to buy something.

g. You wrote a letter to your grandmother, but you didn't put a stamp on it.

COLUMN 1	COLUMN 2
h. Did you write to your grandmother?	o. Yes, but I didn't lock the door.
i. Didn't Tim come to the party last night?	p. Yes, but I didn't buy the coffee.
j. Did your sister drive to work yesterday?	q. Yes, but we didn't like the food very much.
k. Did you go the supermarket yesterday?	r. Yes, but she didn't get my letter.
l. Did you turn off the lights when you went out?	s. Yes, but she didn't get home until ten.
m. Didn't you go to a restaurant last night?	t. Yes, but he didn't stay long.
n. Did your father see a Japanese movie in Tokyo?	u. Yes, but he didn't understand a word.

Find out consequences

Ask and answer with your partner. Match the questions and answers.

a. Did you forget to take your lunch yesterday?
b. Did you get up late today?
c. Did you eat a lot of cake last night?
d. Did you play football in the rain last week?
e. Did you watch TV all night last Tuesday?
f. Did you forget the shopping list yesterday?
g. Did you have a headache last night?

h. Yes, so I had a stomachache.
i. Yes, so I had a headache on Wednesday.
j. Yes, so I had to go to bed early.
k. Yes, so I had lunch in a coffee shop.
l. Yes, so I had to call home.
m. Yes, so I was late for school.
n. Yes, so I caught a cold.

Language Points
Reading and note-taking

Read the article and, on your paper, take notes on the following:

WHO was in the accident?	WHEN did the accident happen?	WHERE did the accident happen?
HOW did the accident happen?	WHO died in the accident?	WHAT injuries did Davies have?
WHAT injuries did the people in the truck have?	HOW LONG was the traffic blocked?	HOW OLD is Davies?

John Davies in road crash!

October 22

Yesterday a man died and John Davies was hurt in a car accident. Davies, 26, known to millions as England's best tennis player, was driving home from the tennis court. It was about 7 p.m. and the traffic on High Street was going about 30 m.p.h.

It was raining, but Davies decided to pass and so he did not see a truck which was coming the other way. The driver of the truck tried to stop but the brakes did not work on the wet road and there was a terrible crash. The car hit the truck and a man who was walking his dog on the sidewalk was struck by the truck and died. Davies was not seriously hurt, although his nose was cut. The people in the truck were bruised but they were not seriously hurt.

There was a terrible traffic jam until 10 p.m.

Writing

1. Make a chart like this. Complete it with your partner.

Main idea	Details	Description of the accident	Consequences

2. Write a short paragraph about the accident.

Listening

Make a chart like this. Then listen to the "Radio News" and fill in your chart.

Type of accident	? ? ? ? ? ? ? ? ? ? ? ? ? ?
Name(s) of people involved	? ? ? ? ? ? ?
Name of road or street	? ? ? ? ? ? ?

Practice Points

1. Copy and complete the following paragraph, using the words in the box. (Each word can be used only once.)

Last . . . at about nine o'clock, Mrs. Nelson was . . . for the . . . on 261st Street. She saw a van at the traffic . . . . The light was . . . . Then a young man in a sports car came . . . Palisade Avenue. He . . . driving very fast, and when he tried to . . . at the traffic light it was too late, so his car . . . the van. The driver of the van was . . . and went to the . . . .

bus	from	hit	hospital	hurt	light	night	red
stop	waiting	was					

2. Match the questions and answers and write them on your paper.

a. What happened last night?

b. Where and when did the accident take place?

c. Were there any witnesses?

d. How was Carlos driving?

e. Was the car at the traffic light a sports car?

f. Didn't Carlos try to stop?

g. Was anybody hurt?

h. He was driving fast.

i. Yes, the driver of the van was hurt.

j. There was a car accident.

k. No, it was a van.

l. On 261st Street, at nine o'clock in the evening.

m. Yes, but it was too late.

n. Yes, there was Mrs. Nelson.

3. Write the dialogues from "Find out consequences" on page 69.

4. Copy and complete the sentences on your paper.

a. We didn't hear the alarm clock, so we . . . .

b. My sister didn't stop at the traffic light, so she had . . . .

c. My father didn't eat dinner, so he . . . .

d. I didn't put a stamp on the letter, so my grandmother . . . .

e. I didn't take the list to the supermarket, so . . . .

Check Points

Communication Points

Ask and answer about past events	Didn't you go to the restaurant last night? Yes, but we didn't like the food very much. Did you write to your grandmother?
Narrate a past event	When you arrived, the young man was calling the garage.
Find out consequences	I forgot to put a stamp on the letter, so my grandmother didn't get it.

1.

Carlos He She	was driving very	fast. slowly.

2.

We You They	were	talking.

3.

I You He She We They	didn't	have time. stop.
	had	an accident. a lot of fun.

4.

Did Didn't	you	go to a restaurant? write to your grandmother?

5.

Yes, so we didn't eat at home. No, but I called her.

Words and Expressions

anybody	fast	hurry	turn off	No kidding!
anything	find	hurt	understand	
caught	garage	list	van	
door	grandmother	lock		
else	happen	rain		
explain	helpful	slowly		

Present—Past

catch—caught
drive—drove
forget—forgot
have/has—had
hit—hit

11 AN OLD COUNTRY

MRS. COOPER: Do you miss England, Tim?

TIM: Oh, not much, really, Mrs. Cooper. New York is great!

MRS. COOPER: Where do you come from, Tim?

TIM: I come from Chesham.

MRS. COOPER: How far is that from London?

TIM: It's not far. About 20 miles.

MRS. COOPER: I see. And how big is it?

TIM: Well, it's a small town.

JOHN: How many people live there?

TIM: About 20,000.

JOHN: Is it very old?

TIM: Well, the town is very old. But lots of the houses are modern.

MRS. COOPER: Almost all the towns in England are old, aren't they, Tim? It's an old country.

TIM: That's right, Mrs. Cooper. In fact, some of the towns and cities are more than two thousand years old.

JOHN: That's old, all right!

Communication Points
Locate places

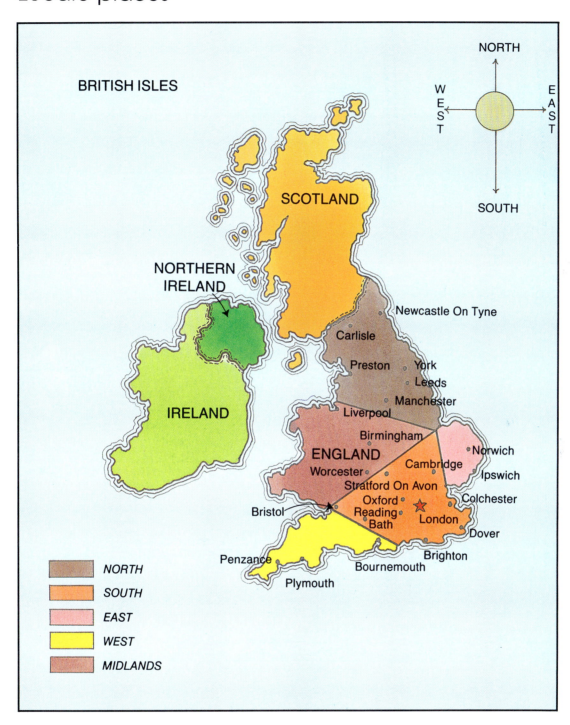

1. **Find the names of five cities from different parts of the map and write them on your paper. Then ask and answer questions about them.**

> A: Where's London?
> B: It's in the south of England.

2. Find the names of five states on the map and write them on your paper. Then ask and answer questions with your partner. Use the list of state name abbreviations to help you.

A: Where's Texas?
B: It's in the Southwest region.

REGIONS OF THE UNITED STATES

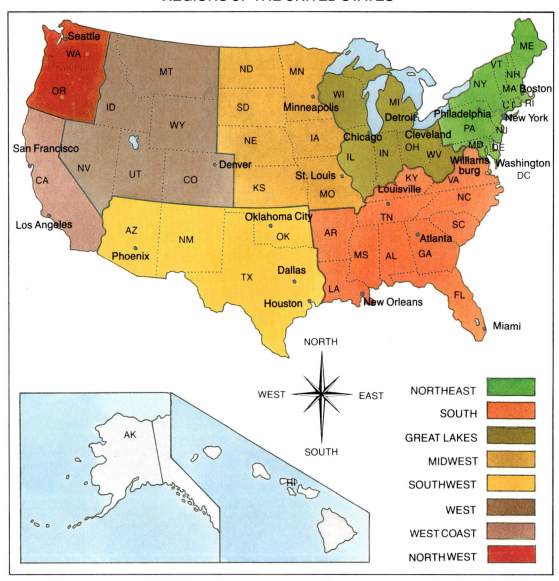

NORTHEAST						
SOUTH						
GREAT LAKES						
MIDWEST						
SOUTHWEST						
WEST						
WEST COAST						
NORTHWEST						

State Name Abbreviations

Alabama	AL	Indiana	IN	Nebraska	NE	South Carolina	SC
Alaska	AK	Iowa	IA	Nevada	NV	South Dakota	SD
Arizona	AZ	Kansas	KS	New Hampshire	NH	Tennessee	TN
Arkansas	AR	Kentucky	KY	New Jersey	NJ	Texas	TX
California	CA	Louisiana	LA	New Mexico	NM	Utah	UT
Colorado	CO	Maine	ME	New York	NY	Vermont	VT
Connecticut	CT	Maryland	MD	North Carolina	NC	Virginia	VA
Delaware	DE	Massachusetts	MA	North Dakota	ND	Washington	WA
Florida	FL	Michigan	MI	Ohio	OH	West Virginia	WV
Georgia	GA	Minnesota	MN	Oklahoma	OK	Wisconsin	WI
Hawaii	HI	Mississippi	MS	Oregon	OR	Wyoming	WY
Idaho	ID	Missouri	MO	Pennsylvania	PA	District of Columbia	DC
Illinois	IL	Montana	MT	Rhode Island	RI		

3. Now find the names of five cities and write them on your paper.
Then ask and answer questions with your partner.

> A: Where's Dallas?
> B: It's in Texas.

Ask and tell where people come from

Ask and answer with your partner. Choose places in England and the
United States.

> A: Where do you come from?
> B: From . . . .
> A: Oh, where's that?
> B: It's in the . . . , near . . . .

Ask and tell about distances

Look at these traffic signs in London. Then ask and answer with your
partner.

¼ mile—a quarter of a mile   1½ miles—one and a half miles
½ mile—half a mile   2 miles—two miles
1 mile—a mile   (1 mile = 1.6 kilometers)

> A: How far is it to Piccadilly Circus?
> B: It's not far. It's just a quarter of a mile away.

> A: How far is it to Marble Arch?
> B: It's quite far. It's two miles away.

Say numbers from 100 to 999

1. Read the numbers.

100	one hundred		500	five hundred
101	one hundred and one		600	six hundred
121	one hundred and twenty-one		700	seven hundred
200	two hundred		800	eight hundred
300	three hundred		900	nine hundred
400	four hundred		999	nine hundred and ninety-nine

2. Take a three day tour of England. Start from London. Look at the map on page 73 and choose five or six cities or towns you would like to visit. Then ask your partner to use the mileage chart to answer your questions.

MILEAGE CHART—ENGLAND

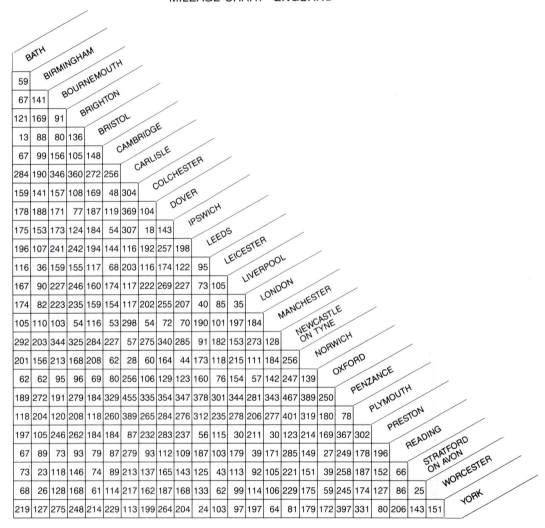

A: How far is it from London to York?
B: It's 197 miles.
A: How far is it from York to Leeds?
B: It's 24 miles.

Say numbers above 1,000

1. Read the numbers.

1,000	one thousand *or* a thousand
1,001	one thousand and one *or* a thousand and one
1,100	one thousand, one hundred *or* eleven hundred
100,000	one hundred thousand *or* a hundred thousand
1,000,000	one million *or* a million
1,100,101	one million, one hundred thousand, one hundred and one.
1,000,000,000	one billion

2. Read these numbers with your partner.

1,150	10,680	220,000	1,500,000
3,000	50,000	450,000	2,000,000
4,500	88,900	900,000	3,750,000
9,750	24,870	748,000	5,000,000

> 1,150   one thousand, one hundred and fifty

3. Take a two week tour of the United States. Start from New York. Look at the map on page 74 and choose six cities or towns you would like to visit. Then ask your partner to use the mileage chart on this page to answer your questions.

MILEAGE CHART—UNITED STATES

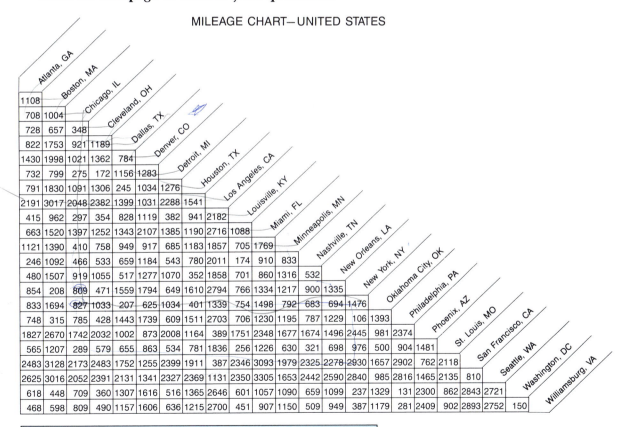

A: How far is it from New York to Chicago?
B: It's 809 miles.
A: How far is it from Chicago to Minneapolis?
B: It's 410 miles.

4. Read the graph and decide how large each town or city is. Then make a chart like the one below and fill it in.

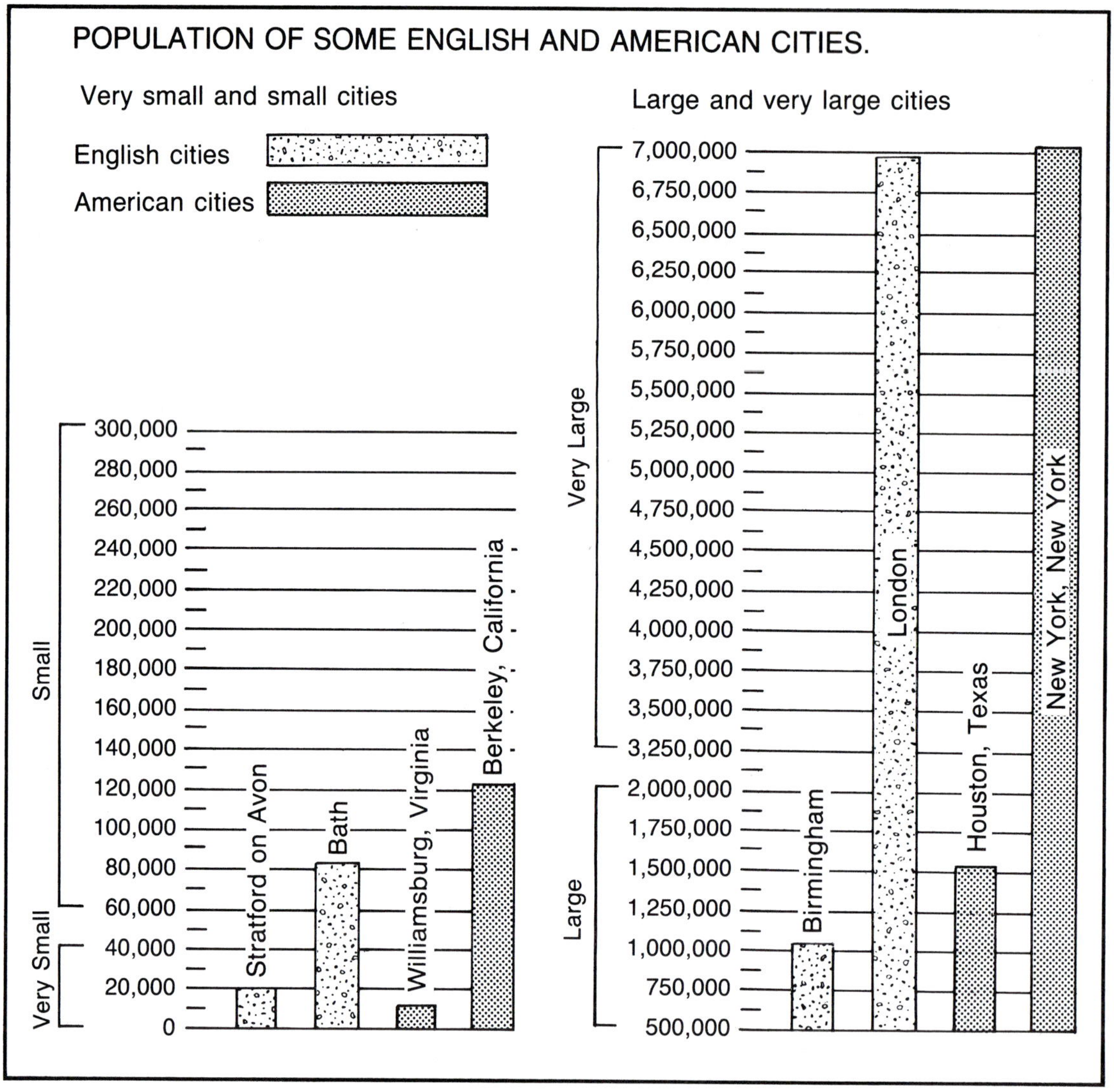

POPULATION OF SOME ENGLISH AND AMERICAN CITIES.

Very small and small cities

English cities

American cities

Large and very large cities

Very Large

7,000,000
6,750,000
6,500,000
6,250,000
6,000,000
5,750,000
5,500,000
5,250,000
5,000,000
4,750,000
4,500,000
4,250,000
4,000,000
3,750,000
3,500,000
3,250,000

London

New York, New York

Small

300,000
280,000
260,000
240,000
220,000
200,000
180,000
160,000
140,000
120,000
100,000
80,000
60,000

Very Small

40,000
20,000
0

Stratford on Avon

Bath

Williamsburg, Virginia

Berkeley, California

Large

2,000,000
1,750,000
1,500,000
1,250,000
1,000,000
750,000
500,000

Birmingham

Houston, Texas

Towns/Cities	Size	Approximate Population
Stratford on Avon	Very small	20,000

5. Ask and answer questions. Use the chart you made in exercise 4.

A: How big is Stratford on Avon?
B: It's very small.
A: How many people live there?
B: About 20,000.

Language Points

Writing

Copy and complete the captions under the pictures. Use the maps on pages 73 and 74 and the chart you made in exercise 4 on page 78 to help you. Each blank can be one word or several words.

1. Stratford on Avon is a *very small* town in the *south* of England. It is the birthplace of Shakespeare and *has* a population of about 20,000.

2. Williamsburg, VA, is a . . . town in the south of the . . . . It was once the capital of Virginia and . . . a . . . of . . . 10,000.

3. Bath is . . . . It is famous for its Roman baths and . . . population . . . about 81,000

4. Berkeley, CA, is . . . , with a . . . of about . . . . It is famous . . . its university.

5. Birmingham is . . . . Its . . . is . . . . It is an industrial city.

6. New York, NY, is . . . . It is an important seaport and . . . 7,071,639.

Reading

Read "London." Then copy and complete the paragraph below.

LONDON

London is the capital of England. It is a huge city and a major port. "The City," which is the original part of London, has an area of about one square mile and a population of 4,580. Greater London is made up of 32 sections and contains nearly seven million people.

London became the capital of England in the Middle Ages but its history goes back more than 2,000 years. London's history attracts tourists from all over the world. Many of these tourists arrive at London's Heathrow Airport, the busiest in Europe. Trains from London's large railroad stations, such as King's Cross, Euston, Paddington, and Victoria, carry millions of passengers each year.

"The City" is the business center of England. Every important company in England, and almost every bank in the world has an office there. London also has two cathedrals, a great abbey, and three universities. It has more theaters, museums, and art galleries than any other city in England. It is also the most important shopping center, with many huge department stores.

Because London is the capital of England, it has many government buildings. It contains the Houses of Parliament, the Prime Minister's House at 10 Downing Street, and Buckingham Palace. People from all over the world go to see "the changing of the guard" each day at Buckingham Palace.

London is . . . of England. It is a huge city and Greater London is made up of . . . with . . . people. The original part is . . . which has an area of only . . . and a population of . . . but which is the . . . center of England. London has a very busy . . . where tourists from . . . arrive and also many . . . from which trains carry millions of passengers. There are also many . . . and many huge . . . . Because London is the capital it has many . . . .

Practice Points

1. Write short dialogues on your paper like the one below.

Tim—England (Chesham)

> A: Where does Tim come from?
> B: He comes from England.
> A: What town does he come from?
> B: Chesham.

   a. Your friends—Japan (Tokyo)
   b. Laura—Mexico (Cuernavaca)
   c. Pablo—Spain (Madrid)
   d. Raul and Luis—Ecuador (Guayaquil)
   e. You— . . . (. . .)

2. Write sentences on your paper about these towns: Preston, Birmingham, Bath, Ipswich, Bristol, Manchester, Plymouth, Penzance. The first one is done for you.

Preston is in the north of England near Manchester.

3. Write dialogues like the one below for the following cities or towns: Williamsburg, VA, Berkeley, CA, Houston, TX. Remember large numbers need commas.

> A: How far is it from New York to . . . ?
> B: It's about . . . miles.
> A: And how big is . . . ?
> B: It's a . . . city.
> A: How many people live there?
> B: About . . . .

4. Write the following numbers in words on your paper.

a. 65,000	b. 125,000	c. 360,000	d. 1,500,000
e. 55,280	f. 2,000,000	g. 21,785	h. 999,999

Check Points

Communication Points

Locate places	Where's Carlisle? It's in the north of England. Where's Dallas? It's in Texas.
Ask and tell where people come from	Where does Tim come from? From Chesham. It's in the south of England, near London.
Ask and tell about distances	How far is it to Marble Arch? It's quite far. It's two miles away.
Say numbers from 100 to 999	401: four hundred and one Dallas is four hundred and one miles from Houston.
Say numbers above 1,000	1,150: one thousand one hundred and fifty

1.

Where	does	he she	come from?
	do	you they	

2.

He She	comes		London. Mexico City. Tokyo. Auckland. New York.
I We They	come	from	

3.

Where's	New York? Atlanta? Houston?

4.

It's in the	Northeast. South. Southwest.

5.

How far is it from London to	York? Worcester? Reading?

6.

It's	197 92 39	miles.

7.

How big is	Stratford-on-Avon? Bath? Houston? New York?

8.

It's	very small. small. large. very large.

9.

How many people live in	Stratford-on-Avon? Bath? Berkeley? New York?

10.

About	20,000. 80,000. 100,000. 7,000,000.

Words and Expressions

almost	hundred	region	numbers 100–999	How big . . .
away	mile	south	numbers 1,000 and above	How far . . .
come	modern	thousand		How many . . .
east	north	town		in fact
graph	people	west		What's it like?
grow	population			
house	quite			

A ROOM FOR RENT 12

PAULO:	Good morning. My name's Paulo Ramirez. I phoned yesterday.
MISS BENNETT:	Oh, yes. Do you want to see the room? Come in, it's down the hall.
MISS BENNETT:	Here we are. As you can see, it's quite a large room. There's a bed, a desk, and a bedside table.
PAULO:	Can I have a stereo?
MISS BENNETT:	Of course. But you have to turn it down after 11:00.
PAULO:	Okay.
MISS BENNETT:	There is an armchair and there are two other chairs.
PAULO:	It looks comfortable.
MISS BENNETT:	Yes. Now, there's a dresser and a closet, so there's plenty of space for clothes.
PAULO:	Are there any bookshelves?
MISS BENNETT:	Yes, there are some bookshelves next to the dresser.
PAULO:	The room's very nice, Miss Bennett. How much is it?
MISS BENNETT:	It's $50 a week.
PAULO:	That sounds okay.
MISS BENNETT:	Good. Now come and have a cup of coffee.
PAULO:	Thank you very much.

Communication Points
Describe a room
Paulo's Room

1. Ask and answer with your partner.

> A: What is in Paulo's room?
> B: There's a bed, a desk . . . . .

2. Ask about your partner's room. Then change roles and let your partner ask about your room.

> A: Is there a desk in your room?
> B: Yes, there is./No, there isn't.
> A: Is there a bedside table?
> B: Yes, there is./No, there isn't.

Miss Bennett's Living Room

3. Ask and answer with your partner.

A: What is in Miss Bennett's living room?
B: There are some chairs, some lamps, ...

4. Ask about your partner's living room.

A: Are there any armchairs in your living room?
B: Yes, there are./No, there aren't./Yes, there's one.
A: Are there any bookshelves?
B: Yes, there are./No, there aren't.

5. Make a list of the furniture in your room, and describe it to your partner.

There's a . . . .
There are some . . . .

Give and refuse permission

1. Read the sign Miss Bennett has posted in Paulo's room.

> ### RULES FOR GUESTS
>
> 1. No noisy or large parties allowed. No loud noise after 11:00 P.M. Turn your radio, TV, stereo down.
>
> 2. Friends are welcome, but let me know in advance. No overnight guests allowed.
>
> 3. Lock the front door at all times.
>
> 4. Use the pay telephone for all calls. Do not use the private phone.
>
> 5. Empty the washing machine and dryer after you use them.
>
> 6. No cooking in the rooms.

2. With your partner, read these dialogues. Which rules answer Paulo's questions?

3. With your partner, give or refuse permission to Paulo. Use the "Rules for Guests" on page 86.

Language Points
Reading
AMERICAN HOUSES

Americans live in many kinds of houses. Many Americans want to live in a single-family house. <u>This</u> is a house that is separated from other houses. <u>It</u> may be large or small, but only one family lives in it. Single family houses are usually in small cities or towns or in the country.

Other Americans live in the big cities. <u>They</u> live in apartments or in rented rooms. Apartment houses often have fifty or more apartments in them. Some apartment houses have elevators that take people to the floor where their apartment is located.

Some Americans live in "townhouses." <u>These</u> are rows of houses joined to each other. Some live in "two-family" houses. A two-family house may be two houses joined together, side by side. <u>It</u> may also be a house with one family on one floor and another family on the floor above.

Almost every house or apartment has a living room and one or more bedrooms. <u>It</u> also has a kitchen and a bathroom. Some houses and apartments have dining rooms.

1. Some words in the reading are underlined. These words refer to or stand for other words in the reading. Work with your partner and decide which words the underlined words refer to or stand for. Then write them on your paper.

2. Complete the descriptions on your paper. Each blank may be one or several words.

a. A single-family house is . . . from . . . .

b. This . . . is two houses . . . together.

c. . . . houses often have . . . in them.

d. . . . are rows of houses . . . .

3. Copy and complete the paragraph on your paper. Each blank may be one or several words.

Almost every house has . . . . It also has . . . . Some houses have . . . .

Practice Points

1. Complete the following sentences on your paper. Use *a, an, some,* or *any*.

    a. What is in your room?
       There's . . . bed, . . . table, and . . . armchair.

    b. Are there . . . bookshelves?
       Well, there aren't . . . in my room, so I have to put . . . of my
       books on the desk.

    c. Do you have . . . cassette recorder?
       No, I don't. But I have . . . stereo.
       Do you have . . . good records?
       Sure! I have . . . Michael Jackson records.

    d. I'm hungry. Are there . . . sandwiches?
       No, there aren't . . . sandwiches, but you can have . . . ice
       cream.

    e. Excuse me! Is there . . . restaurant near here?
       No, there isn't, but there are . . . good restaurants on Third
       Avenue.

    f. Are you thirsty?
       Yes, and I'm hungry, too. Why don't we get . . . root beer
       and . . . couple of hot dogs?

2. Match the questions in the left-hand column with their answers in the right-hand column, and write the dialogues on your paper.

> A: Can I play my stereo at night?
> B: Yes, but you have to turn it down after eleven o'clock.

Questions	Answers
a. Can I play my stereo at night?	g. Okay, but you have to be the catcher.
b. Can I watch TV?	h. Yes, but you have to turn it down after eleven o'clock.
c. Hello, can I speak to Mr. Day?	i. No, you can't, because it's too late. You have to go to bed.
d. Can I go to the movies with Pedro?	j. Yes, but you have to empty them right after you use them.
e. Can I play baseball with you?	k. Sorry, he isn't in. You can't speak to him until tomorrow.
f. Can I use the washing machine and dryer?	l. Yes, you can. But you have to come back early.

Check Points

Communication Points

Describe a room

What is in Paulo's room?
There's a bed, a table, an armchair . . . .
Is there a table in your room? Yes, there is./No, there isn't.
What is in Miss Bennett's living room?
There are some chairs, some lamps . . . .
Are there any lamps in your living room?
Yes, there are./No, there aren't.

Give and refuse permission

Can I listen to the radio? Of course.
Can I make a phone call? Sorry, but you can't use the
    private telephone.
Can I invite some friends?
Of course, but you have to let me know in advance.

1.

What is in	Paulo's	room?
	Miss Bennett's	

2.

There's a	table. closet.
There are some	armchairs. lamps.

3.

Is there a	chair dresser	in your room?
Are there any	armchairs pictures	

4.

Yes, No,	there	is. isn't.
Yes, No,	there	are. aren't.

5.

Can I	listen to the radio? make a phone call? invite some friends? wash my clothes?

6.

Sorry, but you can't	make any noise after 11:00. use the private telephone.
Of course, but you have to	let me know in advance. empty the washing machine.

Words and Expressions

armchair
bedside table
bookshelves
chair
closet
comfortable
desk
downstairs
dresser
dryer
empty
furniture
in advance

invite
lamp
let
make
noise
party
plenty
private
sofa
space
stereo
table
washing machine

dresser
closet
single-family house
two-family house
townhouses

chest of drawers
wardrobe
detached house
semi-detached house
terraced house

A CHICKEN FOR DINNER 13

TIM:	Good morning, Aunt Mary. How are you today?
MISS BENNETT:	Not very well, I'm afraid. I think I'm getting a cold.
TIM:	That's too bad. Is there anything I can do?
MISS BENNETT:	Well, I have to get some things from the store.
TIM:	I can do that. What do you want?
MISS BENNETT:	Let me think . . . I'd like a chicken for dinner.
TIM:	What size do you want? A large one or a small one?
MISS BENNETT:	A small one, please, Tim, and I'd like some cheese.
TIM:	What kind of cheese?
MISS BENNETT:	Cheddar, if they have it.
TIM:	How much do you want?
MISS BENNETT:	Oh, about a pound.
TIM:	Anything else?
MISS BENNETT:	Yes, can you get me some cucumbers, please?
TIM:	Of course! How many?
MISS BENNETT:	Three large ones, I think.
TIM:	Sure. Is that it?
MISS BENNETT:	Yes, thanks, Tim.

(At the supermarket)

TIM:	How much is that, please?
CLERK:	It's $5.79.
TIM:	Here's ten dollars.
CLERK:	Thank you. And here's your change. Have a nice day!
TIM:	You, too! Goodbye.

Communication Points
Make a polite request
Make a choice

1. You are at the farm stand. Take turns with your partner.

A: I'd like some apples, please.
B: Okay. Which ones, red or green?
A: The green ones.
B: How many?
A: Mmm, three, I think.
B: Here you are. That's sixty cents, please.

2. **You also need some things at the supermarket. Make a shopping list from the foods shown below. Be sure to include how much of each item you want. (Americans use different measures from those you may be used to. The chart shows some of these.)**

lb.	= pound	= .454 kilogram	= about ½ kilo
gal.	= gallon	= 3.785 liters	= about 3¾ liters
qt.	= quart	= .946 liter	= about 1 liter
pt.	= pint	= .473 liter	= about ½ liter

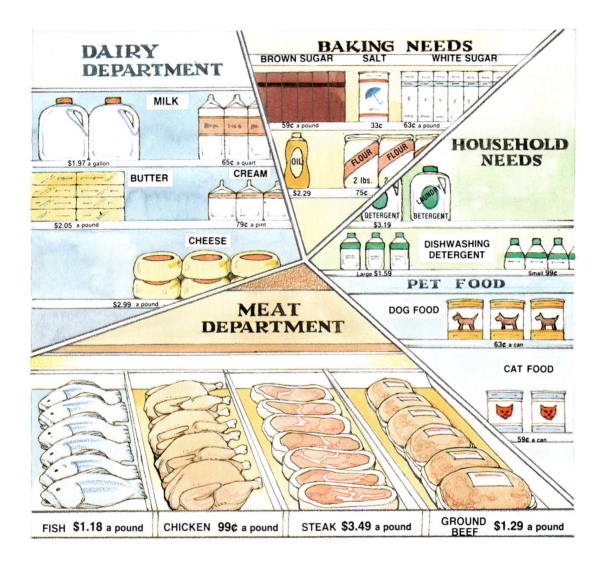

3. **Your partner is going to shop for you. Talk to your partner about the things on your list.**

A: Can you get me some butter, please?
B: How much do you want?
A: A pound.
B: Okay, a pound of butter. What else?
A: . . . .

Language Points
Reading
FOOD IN FLIGHT

a. Walk-in freezer

b. Moving belt

c. Cooking the main dish

d. Roll of hard boiled egg

e. Salads

f. Making breakfast

You're on a plane. The flight attendant asks, "Can I give you some lunch?" You say, "Yes, thank you." Soon you have a tray with a hot lunch, a salad, a roll and butter, and a dessert.

Where do these meals come from? Your lunch starts in the airline office, where food specialists choose the food, make it in their "test kitchens," and write recipes for it.

The menus and recipes then go to an In-flight Food Service, which turns them into meals.

Imagine a "kitchen" as big as a football field. The one in Boston can prepare 11,000 meals a day. This huge kitchen makes meals for many different airlines. "Walk-in" freezers as big as your living room hold boxes of frozen food. The temperature in these rooms is always below zero. You don't stay in there very long!

The first thing we see in the Inflight Food Service building is a moving belt with small food trays on it. As the trays pass by, a worker puts a roll, butter, a salad, and a dessert on each one.

When a tray is full, another worker takes it off the belt and puts it in a cart with shelves just the right size to hold the trays. This cart will later go on the airplane.

The main dish is not on the tray. It is prepared separately. This food is only partly cooked, and then frozen. The airplane's oven finishes the cooking during the flight.

Lettuce for salads is washed and then dried by spinning it in a machine as big as a drum. Slices of hardboiled egg are put on top of the salad to make it look delicious. But these slices did not come directly from an egg. They came from a roll about a foot long, made of cooked egg white on the outside, with a core of cooked egg yolk on the inside.

The space inside a plane is very carefully planned and used. The meal carts fit in special places in the "galley" or kitchen of the airplane. Another cart has everything the flight attendants will need to serve the meal: silverware, the cups and saucers, napkins and coffee pots.

Preparing airline food is a big business. This one kitchen of Inflight Food Service has food worth about $150,000 on hand all the time! People are at work here every day of the year, around the clock. That's what makes it possible for the flight attendant to ask, "Can I give you some lunch?"

g. Meal cart

h. "Can I give you some lunch?"

1. **Read "Food In Flight." Then read each statement and decide if it is true or false. On your paper write the letter of the statement and "true" or "false."**

   a. Inflight Food Service writes the recipes.

   a. false

   b. Inflight Food Service makes meals for more than one airline.
   c. Workers put the main dish for each meal on a moving belt.
   d. Hardboiled eggs are cooked lightly, then frozen.
   e. Lettuce is dried by spinning it in a big machine.
   f. The carts that hold the food are called "galleys."
   g. One of the carts has everything needed to serve meals.

2. **What is the main idea of this reading? Choose the best answer. Be ready to give reasons for your choice.**

   a. Airlines serve thousands of meals every day.
   b. Airlines and Inflight Food Service work together to serve meals to passengers.
   c. Inflight Food Service is open 24 hours a day every day preparing food for airline passengers.
   d. Airline food is partly cooked before it is frozen, and the cooking is finished in the airplane's oven during the flight.

Listening

Listen to the dialogue and write Carol's shopping list on your paper.

Practice Points

1. **Make a chart like the one below. Then look at the words in the box. Write each word in the correct column.**

How Many?	How Much?
apples	butter
bananas	milk
sandwiches	salt

apples	cheese	flour	milk	salt
bananas	cream	flowers	oil	sandwiches
bread	detergent	hot dogs	oranges	sugar
butter	eggs	melons	pumpkins	tomatoes

Now write questions and answers on your paper using *How much?* and *How many?*

How many apples do you want? I'd like three, please.
How much butter do you want? I'd like one pound, please.

2. **Use the information from exercise 1 above to write six short dialogues on your paper like these. Be sure to use a comma before *please.***

A: Can I have some apples, please?
B: How many apples do you want?
A: Three, please.
B: Anything else?
A: No, thank you.

A: Can I have some butter, please?
B: How much butter do you want?
A: One pound, please.
B: Anything else?
A: No, thank you.

3. **There are many ways to make a request. Discuss the differences between the sentences.**

Can I have some sandwiches, please?
I'd like some sandwiches, please.
Carol, pass me the sandwiches.
Give me some sandwiches, please.

4. **Now write sentences on your paper to make requests in the following situations.**

   a. Ask your partner to give you a pen.
   b. Ask the waiter in an expensive restaurant for a piece of cheesecake.
   c. Ask your mother to pass you the milk.
   d. Ask the clerk in a store for a Michael Jackson record.

Check Points

Communication Points

Make a polite request	I'd like some apples, please. Can I have some butter, please?
Make a choice	What size? Large or small? One small one, please. How many apples do you want? Three, please. How much butter do you want? One pound, please.

1.

I'd like	some bananas	please.
Can I have	some butter three apples	please?

2.

Which	one?
	ones?

3.

The	large small	one. ones.

4.

How many	apples oranges tomatoes	do you want?
How much	sugar milk cream	

5.

Three Two Eight	large ones, small ones,	please.
	Two pounds, One quart, One pint,	

Words and Expressions

beef	large	salt	gallon (gal.)	I'd like some . . . .
cream	liquid	sugar	kilo	Anything else?
detergent	melon	steak	kilogram	Is that it?
flour	oil	white	liter	Not very well, I'm afraid.
flower	pumpkin		pint (pt.)	That's too bad.
			pound (lb.)	
			quart (qt.)	

14 A RAINY DAY

JOHN: Wouldn't you know! It's raining again.

TIM: The weather's always bad on Saturday!

JOHN: It sure is! What's the weather like in your country, Tim?

TIM: Well, it changes a lot. Sometimes it's hot, especially in July, and sometimes it's cold. We don't get a lot of snow, but we sure get a lot of fog! It's often very foggy in November.

JOHN: Cold and wet, right? Just like today. Well, what are we going to do now? We sure don't want to go out in this weather. Say, can you play checkers, Tim?

TIM: Checkers? What's that?

JOHN: You know, it's a game you play on a board with round, flat pieces.

TIM: Oh, yes! Draughts. Sure, I can play draughts, but I like chess better. Can you play chess, John?

JOHN: No, I can't. But my dad plays it sometimes.

TIM: Well, I can play very well. Hey, why don't I teach you?

JOHN: Great! I'll go and get the board and the chess pieces.

Communication Points

Talk about the weather

THE FOUR SEASONS IN NEW YORK

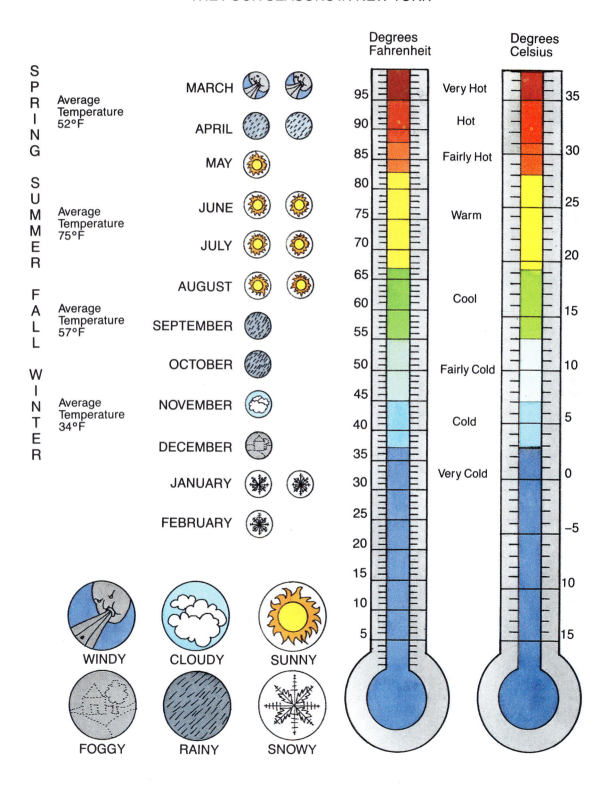

SPRING

Average Temperature 52°F

MARCH
APRIL
MAY

SUMMER

Average Temperature 75°F

JUNE
JULY

FALL

Average Temperature 57°F

AUGUST
SEPTEMBER
OCTOBER

WINTER

Average Temperature 34°F

NOVEMBER
DECEMBER
JANUARY
FEBRUARY

Degrees Fahrenheit

Degrees Celsius

Very Hot
Hot
Fairly Hot
Warm
Cool
Fairly Cold
Cold
Very Cold

WINDY   CLOUDY   SUNNY
FOGGY   RAINY   SNOWY

1. Copy and complete this chart. Use the information on page 99.

The Four Seasons in New York			
Season	Temperature	Weather Conditions Usually	Often
Spring			

2. Ask and answer questions about the weather in New York.

> A: What's the weather like in New York in the spring?
> B: It's cool. It's usually windy in March and rainy in April, but it's often sunny in May.

3. Ask and answer about the weather in your area.

> A: What's the weather like in the spring/summer/fall/winter?
> B: It's . . . .

4. Ask and answer.

> A: What was the weather like yesterday/last week?
> B: It was . . . .

5. Describe the weather in the pictures.

a.

b.

c.

d.

e.

f.

Say what you can do

1. John can play checkers, but he can't play chess. Tim can play checkers, and he also plays chess very well. What can you do? Make your own chart on your paper. Use the following items, and add any others you wish to.

a. sing
b. dance
c. draw
d. play an instrument

e. tell jokes
f. speak English
g. make speeches
h. say tongue twisters

i. solve problems
j. solve puzzles
k. play checkers
l. play chess

m. swim
n. skate
o. play football
p. play baseball

Can you . . .	NO	WELL	VERY WELL
a. sing?	???	???	???
b. dance?			

2. Ask and answer.

> A: Can you sing?
> B: No, I can't./Yes, I can sing very well.
> A: Can you dance?
> B: No, I can't./Yes, I can dance well.

Language Points

Listening

WEATHER FORECAST

Make a chart like this on your paper. Then listen to the weather forecast and fill in the chart. Make eight sections.

Section	Weather	Temperatures High	Low
Northeast	snowy	30	10

Reading

WHAT'S THE WEATHER REPORT?

"Everybody talks about the weather, but nobody does anything about it." An American author wrote these words a hundred years ago, and they are still true today. The weather is a favorite conversation subject. Everybody in America does talk about the weather.

They have a lot to talk about. The United States is so large that it has many kinds of weather at the same time. There can be heavy snow in the Rocky Mountains of the West while it is warm and sunny in Los Angeles and New York City. The weather can be wet and rainy in Texas while it is dry and dusty in Wyoming.

People have always tried to predict the weather. Until modern times, however, their predictions were guesses, based on what the weather was like in other years. Today, weather forecasters use radar, satellite pictures, and com-puters to make their predictions. With these instruments and others, the fore-casters make weather maps each day. The maps show the weather for that day all over the United States.

Some people try to forecast the weather for a whole year or a whole season. Each November, the United States weather service forecasts what the winter will be like. And each year, *The Old Farmer's Almanac* publishes a forecast for the whole year. Both the Weather Service and the *Almanac* use information about past years. They combine this information with obser-vations from satellites, balloons, radar stations, and ships at sea. Then they feed it all into a computer.

Weather reports are very important to Americans. They may not like a lot of their weather, but they certainly like to talk about it.

Read "What's the Weather Report" and answer these questions on your paper.

1. What is the main idea of "What's the Weather Report"?
   a. Everybody in America talks about the weather.
   b. The United States has many kinds of weather at the same time.
   c. Weather forecasters use radar, satellites, and computers.

2. Look at this map. What is the weather in the Northeast region?
   a. rainy   b. snowy   c. sunny   d. cloudy
3. What is the weather in the South?
   a. rainy   b. snowy   c. sunny   d. cloudy
4. Where is the weather cloudy?
   a. West Coast   b. Southwest   c. Great Lakes   d. Midwest

Practice Points

1. Make a chart like this. Fill it in with information about your area.

Season	Temperature	Weather Conditions Usually	Often
Spring	???	???	???

2. Use this information to write sentences like these.

It is quite warm in spring. It is usually windy in March, and is often rainy in April and May.

3. Use the chart below to write sentences on your paper.

Carol can sing, but she can't dance. What about Janet?

	Carol	Janet	Bill	John	Carlos	Deborah	Mark	Neil	David	Paul
sing	yes	no								
dance	no	yes								
draw			yes	no						
play an instrument			no	yes						
speak French					yes	no				
speak Italian					no	yes				
play checkers							no	yes		
play chess							yes	no		
play football									no	yes
play tennis									yes	no

4. Write the questions with their answers. Be sure to use a comma after *No* and *Yes*.

> A: Can you drive a car when you are fourteen?
> B: No, but you can drive a car when you are sixteen.

a. Can you drive a car when you are fourteen?
b. Can Elly play the guitar now?
c. Can you ride your bike here?
d. Can we play baseball?
e. Can John play the guitar?
f. Can you drive a car?
g. Can you ride a bike?
h. Can you play baseball?

i. No, I can't. There's a sign saying no bike riding in the park.
j. No, she has to do her homework first.
k. Yes, we can play baseball in the park.
l. No, I can't drive a car but I can pilot a plane.
m. Yes, he can. He can play very well.
n. Of course I can. I play baseball a lot.
o. No, but you can drive a car when you are sixteen.
p. No, I can't ride a bike very well.

Check Points

Communication Points

Talk about the weather
What's the weather like in the spring?
It's cool. It's usually windy in March and rainy in April but it's often sunny in May.
What was the weather like yesterday? It was cold.

Say what you can do
Can you sing? No, I can't./Yes, I can.

1.
What's the weather like in the	spring? summer? fall? winter?

2.
It's	(very) cold. cool. warm. (very) hot.

3.
It's	usually often	rainy snowy sunny windy cloudy foggy	in	January. February. March. April. May. June.

4.
What was the weather like	yesterday? last week?

5.
It was	(very) cold. cool. warm. (very) hot.

6.
Can you	sing? dance? tell jokes? play chess?

7.
Yes, I can	sing dance tell jokes play chess	well. very well.

8.
No, I can't	sing. dance. tell jokes. play chess.

Words and Expressions

average	cool	instrument	sing	tongue-twister	. . . , right?
bad	draw	joke	snowy	warm	Wouldn't you know!
board	especially	problem	solve	weather	
checkers	fairly	puzzle	speech	windy	
chess	flat	rainy	sunny		
chess pieces	foggy	say	teach		
cloudy	hot	season	tell		

checkers   draughts

GOOD LUCK MIGUEL

JANET: Do you really have to go back to Mexico tomorrow, Miguel?

MIGUEL: Yes, I do. My father has to work in Mexico City for a while. He went back last week.

TIM: What time are you going?

MIGUEL: Early in the morning.

JOHN: How early, Miguel?

MIGUEL: I have to be at the airport by seven.

JANET: How are you going to get there?

MIGUEL: Mr. Day is going to take me.

CAROL: Miguel, you *are* going to come back, aren't you?

MIGUEL: Of course! I'm coming back next summer, I hope. My father is going to work in New York again, and I'm going to come here with him.

BILL: Well, don't forget to write.

MIGUEL: I won't forget. I'm going to write everybody! And thanks for the present.

Communication Points
Talk about your plans

1. **Make an appointment book page on your paper for a week when there's no school. Write your plans for that week. Here are some suggestions. Leave two mornings and two afternoons free.**

play tennis	go to the dentist's	go swimming
go shopping	have a party	wash the car
watch the ball game	visit my grandparents	go fishing

Make your page like this.

APRIL	
MORNING	**AFTERNOON**
2 SUNDAY ??	??
3 MONDAY ??	??
4 TUESDAY ??	
5 WEDNESDAY ??	
6 THURSDAY ??	
7 FRIDAY ??	
8 SATURDAY	

2. **Arrange to meet your partner on a free morning or afternoon.**

> A: Can we meet on Sunday morning?
> B: Sorry, but I'm playing tennis on Sunday morning./Yes, I'm free on Sunday morning.

3. **Arrange to meet other students. Try to make appointments for all your free mornings and afternoons.**

Ask and tell what people are going to do

Stuart MacDuff, Sue's brother, is going to spend a weekend in New York and wants to go sightseeing on Saturday. He is going to stay in a hotel at 7th Avenue and 33d Street. Sue is going to meet him there on Saturday morning. Here is the sightseeing plan she has prepared.

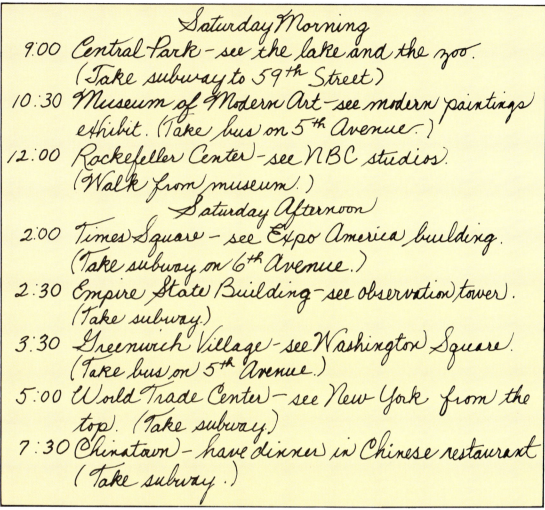

Saturday Morning

9:00 Central Park – see the lake and the zoo. (Take subway to 59th Street)

10:30 Museum of Modern Art – see modern paintings exhibit. (Take bus on 5th Avenue.)

12:00 Rockefeller Center – see NBC studios. (Walk from museum.)

Saturday Afternoon

2:00 Times Square – see Expo America building. (Take subway on 6th Avenue.)

2:30 Empire State Building – see observation tower. (Take subway.)

3:30 Greenwich Village – see Washington Square. (Take bus on 5th Avenue.)

5:00 World Trade Center – see New York from the top. (Take subway.)

7:30 Chinatown – have dinner in Chinese restaurant. (Take subway.)

1. **Ask and answer with your partner.**

> A: What is Stuart going to see first?
> B: Central Park.
> A: When is he going to see it?
> B: At nine o'clock.
> A: What is he going to do there?
> B: He's going to see the lake and the zoo.
> A: How is he going to get there?
> B: By subway.
> A: What is he going to see then?
> B: . . . .

2. **Look at Sue's plan, and write on your paper everything Stuart is going to do.**

   At 9:00, Stuart is going to see the lakes and the zoo in Central Park. At 10:30...

Language Points
Reading and writing
SIGHTSEEING IN NEW YORK

Here are pictures and descriptions of some places you can visit in New York. Imagine you are going to spend a day there, and write a plan similar to Sue's plan on page 107. Choose all the places you want to see, and write them on your paper, with the times and the things you will do there.

Rockefeller Center

Rockefeller Center is on 5th and 6th Avenues between 48th and 51st Streets. In the winter, there are crowds around the outdoor ice-skating rink at Rockefeller Center. In the summer, the rink becomes an outdoor restaurant. There are many other things to do, because Rockefeller Center is the largest entertainment and business complex in the world. It is the home of Radio City Music Hall, where long lines of people wait to see the famous chorus line of dancers, the Rockettes, and it contains the NBC television studios.

Staten Island Ferry

The Staten Island Ferry leaves from Battery Park at the southern tip of Manhattan Island. On a hot summer day you can cool off by taking this ferry, a boat that makes regular trips from Manhattan to Staten Island. As soon as the ferry moves out into the harbor you can feel the strong ocean breeze. It's delightful! And the ferry is still very cheap; it's only 25 cents.

The Empire State Building

The best way to get a look at Manhattan is to go up to the top of the Empire State Building. From the Observation Deck on the 102nd floor you can look down in all directions. The East River is on one side and the Hudson River on the other. The large green square of Central Park spreads across the center of the island. There are telescopes for visitors to use. And of course there are tiny Empire State Buildings to buy as souvenirs. The Empire State Building is on 5th Avenue at 34th Street.

The Statue of Liberty

The Statue of Liberty is in New York harbor. To get there, you take a boat from Battery Park, at the southern tip of Manhattan Island. The lamp held high by the figure of Liberty has very special meaning to Americans. A great wave of immigrants arrived in New York in the early 1900's and were welcomed by the Statue of Liberty. Every hour crowded ferries take visitors out to Liberty Island. On the island you can climb up in the statue right up into the crown.

Central Park

This large park is in the middle of Manhattan. It lies between 5th and 8th Avenues, and between 59th and 110th Streets. It has gardens, a lake, playgrounds, a theater, and a zoo. At the southern corner of the park there are horse-drawn carriages. Along the edge is an endless market of people selling everything from books to belts and flowers to footwear. At the eastern edge is the Metropolitan Museum of Art, and to the west is the Museum of Natural History.

Listening

Sue and Barbara are in a restaurant. They are sitting at a table and drinking coffee. Listen to them talking and answer the following questions on your paper.

a. What are Sue and Barbara going to do?
b. When are they going to leave?
c. How are they going to get there?
d. What are they going to do in the morning?
e. What are they going to do in the evening?
f. When are they going to come back?

Practice Points

1. Rewrite these sentences on your paper using the correct form of the word in parentheses.

I (have) a party next Saturday. Do you want to come?

I am having a party next Saturday. Do you want to come?

a. Sue (arrive) tomorrow morning. Can you meet her at the airport?
b. What's the time, please? I (meet) John at half past eight.
c. Sorry, but I can't come. I (take) my mother to the dentist's.
d. We (go) to the movies this evening. Why don't you do your homework now?
e. Sorry, but I can't meet you Tuesday afternoon. I (see) the doctor at four o'clock.
f. Miguel (leave) at eight o'clock tomorrow. Can we meet him at seven?
g. Barbara and Sue (go) shopping. Tell them to buy some cheese and some butter.

2. Look at these schedules.

This is what Bill does every day . . .

. . . and this is what he is going to do tomorrow, because it's Sunday.

Every Day	
7:30	gets up
7:45	has breakfast
8:35	arrives at school
8:45	school starts
12:30	has lunch at school
3:20	gets home
6:30	has dinner at home
7:15	does homework
8:00	watches TV
9:45	goes to bed

Tomorrow (Sunday)	
9:00	get up
9:30	have breakfast
10:00	play baseball
1:00	have lunch at home
3:00	visit the Statue of Liberty with John
6:30	have supper at home
7:00	read an adventure story
8:00	watch TV
10:30	go to bed

3. Write on your paper what Bill did yesterday. Be sure to use a colon (:) when you write the time.

Yesterday Bill got up at 7:30. Then he....

4. Now write what Bill is going to do tomorrow (Sunday).

Tomorrow Bill is going to get up at 9:00.

5. Write answers for the following questions. The first one is done for you.

    a. When is Miguel going to leave? (early in the morning)

Miguel is going to leave early in the morning.

    b. How is he going to get to the airport? (Mr. Day)
    c. When are they going to meet them? (on Thursday)
    d. What are you going to see at Rockefeller Center? (the NBC studios)
    e. Where is Sue going to go next week? (to Toronto)
    f. What are you going to do today? (stay at home)
    g. When are they going to mail the letter? (tomorrow morning)
    h. How are they going to get to the Museum? (by bus)
    i. What is John going to do in the afternoon? (meet Bill)

Check Points

Communication Points

Talk about your plans	Can we meet on Sunday morning? Sorry, but I'm playing tennis on Sunday morning./Yes, I'm free on Sunday morning.
Ask and tell what people are going to do	What is Stuart going to see first? Central Park. When is he going to see it? At nine o'clock. What is he going to do there? He's going to see the lake and the zoo. How is he going to get there? By subway. What is he going to do then? He's going to . . . .

1.

I'm	free playing tennis going to the dentist's doing homework meeting Stuart going fishing having a party	on	Sunday Monday Tuesday Wednesday Thursday Friday Saturday	morning. afternoon. evening.

2.

What is	Stuart he she	going to	see do	first? then? there?

3.

He's She's	going to	see	the lake. a painting exhibition. Washington Square.
			have dinner in a restaurant.

4.

When is	he she	going to see it?	At	9:00. 10:30. 12:00.

5.

6.

How is	he she	going to get there?	By	bus. subway.

7.

Words and Expressions

exhibit grandparents	painting	I'm free on . . . .

16 GOING HOME

ATTENDANT:	Can I get you anything to drink?
MIGUEL:	Yes, I guess I'll have something. What do you have?
ATTENDANT:	Let's see. We have coffee, tea, and milk, and we have cola, ginger ale, and orange . . .
MIGUEL:	I'll have some ginger ale, please.
ATTENDANT:	Here you are.
MIGUEL:	Thanks. Oh, can you tell me when the plane will arrive in Mexico City?
ATTENDANT:	In about four hours. We'll arrive at 10 o'clock.
MIGUEL:	Thank you.
ATTENDANT:	You're welcome. Are you going to stay in Mexico City?
MIGUEL:	Well, no. I'm going to Toluca.
ATTENDANT:	Toluca? Is that far from Mexico City?
MIGUEL:	No, I'll get there in about an hour if there's not too much traffic.
ATTENDANT:	Traffic's always a problem, isn't it? We even have traffic jams in the sky sometimes! But I don't think we'll have one today.

Communication Points
Make requests
State intentions

1. Ask and answer with your partner.

> A: Will you take us for a ride?
> B: Yes, I will. I'll take you for a ride this afternoon.

... take us for a ride (this afternoon)

... go to the dance with me (tonight)

... take Mother to the movies (Friday)

... wash the car (tomorrow)

2. Miss Bennett is going to stay with a friend in Albany for a week. She is asking Tim to look after the house. With your partner, take the roles of Miss Bennett and Tim.

> MISS BENNETT: You won't forget to lock the door, will you?
> TIM: Don't worry, I won't. I'll lock the door every night.

... lock the door (every night)

... feed the cat (every day)

... water the plants (every morning)

... check the mail (every day)

Make decisions

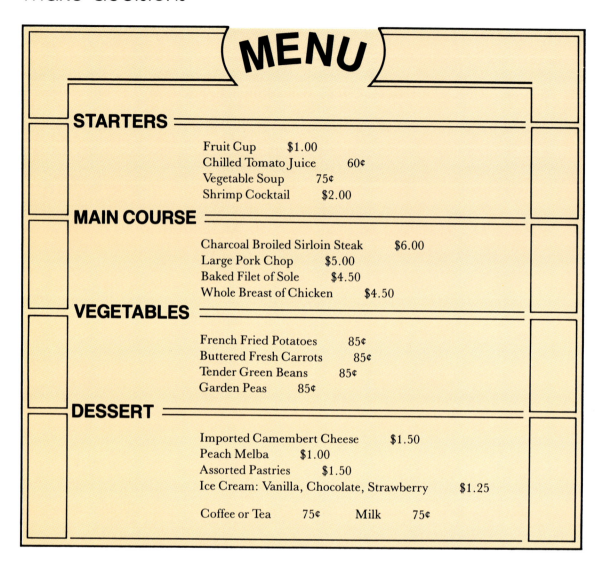

MENU

STARTERS

Fruit Cup $1.00
Chilled Tomato Juice   60¢
Vegetable Soup   75¢
Shrimp Cocktail $2.00

MAIN COURSE

Charcoal Broiled Sirloin Steak $6.00
Large Pork Chop $5.00
Baked Filet of Sole $4.50
Whole Breast of Chicken $4.50

VEGETABLES

French Fried Potatoes   85¢
Buttered Fresh Carrots   85¢
Tender Green Beans   85¢
Garden Peas   85¢

DESSERT

Imported Camembert Cheese $1.50
Peach Melba $1.00
Assorted Pastries $1.50
Ice Cream: Vanilla, Chocolate, Strawberry $1.25

Coffee or Tea   75¢   Milk   75¢

Open dialogue

You invited your partner to dinner at a restaurant. Look at the menu and decide what you want to eat. Then do the open dialogue with your partner.

A: Anything to start with? There's . . . .
B: Yes, I'll have . . . ./No, nothing for me, thanks.
A: Well, I think I'll have . . . .
Now, what about the main course? They have . . . .
B: . . . .
A: Any vegetables with it? There are . . . .
B: . . . .
A: Good, I'll have the . . . . and some . . . .
What about dessert? There's . . . .
B: . . . .
A: That sounds super! I'm going to have some, too.
Something to drink? They have . . . .
B: . . . .
A: Okay. I'll have . . . .
Oh, good! The waiter's coming.

Make predictions
Listening

1. **Make a chart like this on your paper. Then listen to the four conversations and fill in the chart.**

	Tim	Airplane captain	Mr. & Mrs. Day	Miss Bennett
Means of travel	bus	????	????	????
Destination	Hyde Park	????	????	????
Time	9:00	???		
Time of arrival	11:00			

2. **Ask and answer questions with your partner.**

> A: Where's Tim?
> B: He's on a bus.
> A: Where's he going?
> B: He's going to Hyde Park.
> A: When will he arrive?
> B: He'll arrive in two hours.

Preflight check

Language Points
Reading
UP, UP, AND AWAY!

A jet plane streaks across the sky, leaving a long, straight trail of white cloud. You look at it and wish you were in the pilot's seat. You wonder how you can get into flying.

One answer is an air cadet program. In the United States, and in many other countries, air cadet programs help young people learn about flying.

The American program is the Civil Air Patrol Cadet Program. The CAP is a volunteer group of 70,000 Americans of all ages. It has 6,000 planes that belong to individual members, and its most important work is "search and rescue." CAP volunteers look for people who are lost in the mountains or the desert, and they help in disasters such as floods or hurricanes.

The Air Cadet Program is another important part of the CAP's work. It is open to young Americans of both sexes who either have finished the 6th grade or are at least 13. Cadets can stay in the program until they are 21. There are about 25,000 CAP cadets at present, learning about aviation on their weekends.

What do they do? They take flight training classes, first aid and life saving, and they learn survival and rescue techniques. They get "hands-on" experience in CAP aircraft, and study navigation, weather, and aviation history. Cadets can compete for flying and academic scholarships. In one recent year, more than $40,000 of scholarship money was awarded to CAP cadets.

Two-week programs each year bring groups of cadets together at an air base to work toward a special goal. One year, 16 cadets from Minnesota worked toward their first solo flights. For fun, they gave an award each day to the cadet who made the biggest "goof-up" or silly mistake. One cadet won by trying to start the plane's engine with the starter in the Off position. Another winner tried to take off while the plane's tail was still tied down. All 16 cadets soloed successfully.

Each year, more than 100 American cadets go to other countries in an International Air Cadet Exchange Program, and air cadets come to the United States from other countries. International understanding and friendship grow as these students from different nations share their love for flying.

The air cadet program: a way to get "up, up, and away." Could it be your gateway into the world of aviation?

Radio check before a search mission

Cadets at Air and Space Museum, Washington, D.C.

Cadet receives Outstanding award for first-time attendance at an encampment.

1. **Read "Up, Up, and Away." Then write five questions on your paper about the reading and ask your partner to answer them.**

2. **Think about these questions and be ready to discuss them in class.**

   a. The Minnesota group had a "goof-up" award. Can you think of two goof-ups of your own? What kinds of goof-ups might happen in your class?

   b. What kinds of scholarships can CAP cadets try for? What other kinds of scholarships are there?

   c. Do you know anyone who owns his or her own plane? Why do people own planes? What do they use them for?

   d. Look at the list of things that CAP cadets study. Why do you think each of these subjects was chosen? What other subjects can you suggest for cadets to study?

Practice Points

1. Copy and complete each sentence on your paper, using *something, anything*, or *nothing*.

    a. I'm thirsty; I think I'll have . . . to drink.
    b. Let's have . . . to start with. There's onion soup and shrimp cocktail.
    c. I won't have . . . for dessert.
    d. I was thirsty, but he didn't have . . . for me to drink.
    e. I didn't have supper; there was . . . to eat in the house.
    f. I didn't have . . . to eat; I only had a cup of coffee.
    g. I'm broke now, so I can't buy . . . else.
    h. I'm sorry, I'm afraid there's . . . I can do about it now.

2. Agree to do something. On your paper, write what you say.

    a. Carol and Janet want to ride in Patricia's car. Agree to take them for a ride.

        I'll take you for a ride this afternoon.

    b. You are leaving. Agree to write soon.
    c. Miss Bennett is leaving. Agree not to forget to water her plants.
    d. Bill wants to meet you. Agree to phone him tomorrow.
    e. The Coopers will arrive at eight o'clock. Agree to meet them.
    f. Your mother wants to go to the movies. Agree to take her there tonight.

3. Write answers to these questions.

    a. Where will you be tomorrow night? (at home)

        I'll be at home.

    b. When will the plane arrive? (at 2:30)
    c. How will he get to the airport? (by subway)
    d. What time will you go to bed tonight? (at eleven o'clock)
    e. How will you go to the museum tomorrow? (by bus)
    f. When will they come back again? (in March)
    g. Where will Sue and Barbara go next weekend? (to the beach)
    h. What will you have for breakfast? (scrambled eggs)

4. Make decisions and write sentences about them.

    a. It's raining. Decide not to play tennis.

        It's raining. I won't play tennis.

    b. You're hungry. Decide to have a sandwich and a glass of milk.
    c. There's too much traffic this morning. Decide to walk to school.
    d. You're tired. Decide not to stay out late tonight.
    e. You're not feeling well. Decide not to go to school today.
    f. There's nothing interesting on TV. Decide to go to the movies.
    g. Bob is late. Decide not to wait for him this time.

5. Write answers to these questions. The first one is started for you.

a. What time will you get up tomorrow morning?

I'll get up at...

b. What will you do then?
c. What time will you go to school?
d. How will you get there?
e. What time will you finish school?
f. What time will you get home?
g. What will you do after dinner?
h. What time will you go to bed?

Check Points

Communication Points

Make requests	Will you take us for a ride? Yes, I'll take you for a ride this afternoon.
State intentions	You won't forget to lock the door, will you? Don't worry, I won't. I'll lock the door every night.
Make decisions	Anything to start with? There's fruit cup, chilled tomato juice, vegetable soup, and shrimp cocktail.
Make predictions	When will Tim arrive? He'll arrive at eleven o'clock.

1.

When will	Tim Miss Bennett Mr. and Mrs. Wilde	arrive?

2.

He She They	will arrive	in two hours. half an hour.
		at eleven o'clock.

3.

Will you	take us for a ride? go to the dance with me? wash the car? take Mother to the movies?

4.

Yes, I will. I'll	take you for a ride go to the dance with you wash the car take Mother to the movies	this afternoon. tonight. tomorrow. the day after tomorrow.

5.

You won't forget to	lock the doors, feed the cat, water the plants, wind the clock,	will you?

6.

Don't worry, I won't.

7.

Do you want	something anything	to eat?

8.

Yes, please. No, nothing for me, thanks.

Words and Expressions

attendant	chilled	peach melba	starter	That sounds super!
baked	feed	plant	traffic	
beans	finish	potato	traffic jam	
buttered	imported	shrimp cocktail	vanilla	
breast of chicken	main course	sirloin steak	worry	
broiled	pastries	sky		
carrot	pea	soon		

Sing a song!

TAKE ME HOME, COUNTRY ROADS by Bill Danoff, Taffy Nivert, John Denver

Words and Expressions

Numbers refer to the units in which words and expressions are introduced.

population	11	sing	14	summer	7	understand	10
postcard	4	single-family		sunny	14	us	9
potato	16	house	12	sure	2	use	2
pound (lb.)	13	sirloin steak	16	swim	5	usually	5
private	12	sit	2	table	12	vacation	7
problem	14	ski	5	take	3	van	10
pumpkin	13	slowly	10	teach	14	vanilla	16
puzzle	14	snowy	14	teeth	5	vegetable	5
quart (qt.)	13	sofa	12	tell	14	waist	9
quite	11	solve	14	them	9	walk	2
rain	10	sometimes	5	these	2	warm	14
rainy	14	soon	16	third	3	wash	4
receptionist	9	sore	9	those	2	washing	
region	11	south	11	thousand	11	machine	12
right	3	space	12	throat	9	wear	1
sail	6	speech	14	toe	9	weather	14
salad	5	sports	7	together	4	weekend	7
salt	13	spring	7	tongue-twister	14	welcome	1
say	14	stadium	5	tooth	9	west	11
season	14	stairs	4	touch	9	when	5
second	3	stamps	4	town	11	white	13
send	4	steak	13	townhouses	12	why	2
serious	9	stereo	12	traffic	16	windy	14
ship	7	stomachache	9	traffic jam	16	winter	7
shoulder	9	stop	8	traffic light	3	worry	16
shrimp		story	6	travel	4	write	8
cocktail	16	straight	1	turn off	10	x-rays	9
sick	9	study	4	twice	5		
side	2	sugar	13	two-family			
sign	2	supermarket	4	house	12		

Expressions

Anything else?	13	No problem.	1
Can I help You?	4	Not very well, I'm afraid.	13
Can you do me a favor?	1	Oh, my gosh!	9
Don't worry.	9	Over there . . .	4
Great!	6	. . ., sir.	2
Here I am.	8	. . ., right?	14
How about . . .?	6	spare time	5
How big . . .?	11	Thanks a lot.	1
How far . . .?	11	That sounds super!	16
How many . . .?	11	That's too bad.	13
I'd/you'd/he'd/she'd/		Wait a minute.	1
we'd/they'd better . . .	9	Watch out!	8
I'd like some . . .	13	What about . . .?	6
I'm free on . . .	15	What's it like?	11
I'm sorry.	2	What's wrong with	
in fact . . .	11	her/him?	9
Is that it?	13	Wouldn't you know!	14
It's pretty far.	3	You can't miss it.	3
Let me know in advance	12	What can I do for you?	6
Let's have a look.	9		
Let's see . . .	1	**Number Names**	
Make the bed.	7		
My pleasure.	5	100–999	11
No kidding!	10	1,000 and above	11

Appendix

Words and Expressions introduced in *Turning Points 1*.

a
add
address
Afghan
afternoon
again
airplane
all
alone
alphabet
American
an
and
answer
anywhere
am
apple
are
art
at
ball
banana
baseball
basketball
bat
bathroom
batter
be
beautiful
bed
bedroom
bench
bicycle
big
bike
bird
book
bottom
bowl
bread
brother
builder
bus
bus stop
but
butter
cake
camera
can
Canadian
canaries
can't
car
card
cards
cartoons
cassette recorder

cat
cent
cheap
check
cheese
cheesecake
chicken
children
Chinese
city
class
classical music
clock
clothes
club
coffee
cola
color
comedies
comics
computer
  programmer
concert
cookies
country
cover
cup
cut
Dad
dance
dancer
daughter
detective stories
diamond
did
dime
dining room
disco
do
doctor
dog
dollar
doughnuts
down
drink
drums
early
eat
editor
eggs
engineer
English
evening
expensive
family
fans
fantastic

far
farmer
fat
father
favorite
film
fine
folk music
food
football
football field
football game
for
friends
from
fruit
frying pan
German
get up
give
glass
go
goldfish
golfer
good
got up
grapes
great
grilled
growl
guitar
half
hall
hamburger
hamster
hat
have
he
heat
help
her
here
here's (here is)
he's (he is)
him
his
hit
home
home run
homework
horror films
hospital
hot chocolate
hot dogs
hungry
husband
I

ice cream
idea
I'm (I am)
in
invitation
is
it
Italian
Japanese
jazz
kind
kitchen
know
lake
last name
late
lawyer
lemonade
lesson
letter
library
like
listen
live
living room
look
low
magazine
mechanic
meet
meeting
melt
menu
Mexican
milk
milkshakes
Miss
month
mother
motorcycle
movies
Mr.
Mrs.
my
mystery
name
nationality
near
newspaper
nickel
night
no
not
now
o'clock
of
often

old
on
only
orange juice
organ
our
out
painter
park
park (a car)
parrot
pass
past
pastry
pear
pen
penny
pets
phone booth
phone number
photographer
piano
pickles
picnic
picture
pie
piece
pilot
pizza
plate
play
played
police officer
pony
pop music
post office
poster
prefer
present
put
quarter
radio
read
ready
record
record player
restaurant
reporter
rice
ride
road
rock music
romantic
room
root beer
run
same

sandwich
saw
school
science
science fiction
see
she
she's (she is)
shop
short
singer
sister
skate
slice
small
so
soccer
soda
some
something
son
soup

spaghetti
Spanish
speak
spell
start
stay
stayed
stories
street
student
stupid
subway station
supper
sweater
taco
talk
tall
tea
teacher
team
tennis match
telephone

that
the
theater
their
them
there
they
thin
think
thirsty
this
throw
time
tired
to
today
tomato
tomorrow
tonight
too
top
train

truck
trumpet
T-shirt
turn
turtles
TV
typewriter
up
very
visit
wait
waiter
was
watch
watched
water
we
wear
week
well
went
were

western
what's (what is)
where
which
who
wife
window
with
woman
work
write
yard
yes
yesterday
yogurt
you
young
your
you're (you are)
zoo

Expressions

a couple of
a friend of mine
all evening
all right
a lot of fun
as usual
At last!
Bye!
Bye, you guys!
Come in.
Come on!
do the dishes
Excuse me.
Gee. . . .
Good afternoon.
Good-bye.
Good evening.
Good morning.
Good night.
Great idea!
Happy Birthday!
Have a good time!
Hello!
Here you are.
Hey, look!
Hey, you guys!
Hi!
Hold on a minute.
How about you?
How are you?
How do you do?
How much?
How much is it
  all together?
How nice.
How old are you?

Hurry up!
I don't know.
I don't think so.
I'm a little . . .
I'm broke.
I mean . . .
I must hurry now.
I'm not too young . . .
in fact
I see.
Keep your eye on the ball.
Let's go.
Let's go/get . . .
Let's go look at it.
Look at him go!
looks like
lots of
never mind
Nice to meet you.
No, thanks.
Nothing special.
of course
Oh, gosh!
Oh, I see.
Oh, really?
Oh, sure.
Oh, thanks.
Okay
over there
Please
right now
See you. . .
See you later.
See you soon.
See you tomorrow.
so long

strike out
Take care!
thanks
Thank you.
That's a pity.
That's right.
They're something else!
watch TV
What about . . . ?
What are you doing?
What else?
What time is it?
Well, . . .
Why don't we . . . instead?
Wow!
Yes, I do.
Yes, please.
You do?
You're right.
You're up!
You're welcome.

Number Names

1–12
13–23
30–90

Color Names

black	pink	orange
blue	red	
brown	white	
green	yellow	

Days
Months